⁓∴ Kilkenny ∴⁓

City and County

Text by Gerry Moran

Paintings by Ann Phelan

Cottage

Publications

The Author

Gerry Moran was born and raised in Kilkenny. He attended the CBS Primary and Secondary schools and is a graduate of UCD and St. Patrick's Training College, Drumcondra. He is the former Principal of St. Patrick's Boys Primary School, in Kilkenny.

Gerry writes a weekly column for the *Kilkenny People* newspaper, is a regular contributor to RTE's *Sunday Miscellany* (Radio 1), and contributes to a variety of publications.

A former president of Kilkenny Toastmasters Club, he won the Toastmasters International Humorous Speech competition in 1990.

Gerry has a keen interest in the history of his native city and is a member of the Kilkenny Archaeological Society.

He lives with wife and family in Kilkenny.

The Artist

Ann Phelan (née Sheehan) was born in Wexford in 1958. She studied advertising in the College of Commerce, Rathmines, Dublin.

After leavng college, she worked in Dublin for a number of years, before returning to Wexford and meeting her fututre husband Liam. They moved to Kilkenny 23 years ago, and have one son, Liam Anthony.

Ann is a self taught artist, and her preferred mediums are watercolour, acrylic and oils. Buildings and gardens are her favourite subjects, and she has been painting for the last 17 years, with many exhibits in Kilkenny over the years.

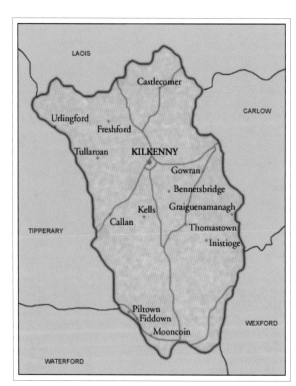

Co. Kilkenny

Contents

Kilkenny - a Brief History

The writer Frank O'Connor described Kilkenny as 'the loveliest of Irish counties'. Situated in the 'sunny south-east' of Ireland, this small compact county is over 64 km long, 32 km broad, and has a population of 87,558.

The main towns and villages of Kilkenny, by population (Census 2006) are: Kilkenny City and environs (22,179), Thomastown (1837), Callan (1771), Castlecomer (1531), Graiguenamanagh (1376), Ballyragget (1014), Mooncoin (1002), Piltown (968), Urlingford (867), Freshford (734) and Bennetsbridge (685).

Kilkenny County is low-lying. The hills are not too high, the valleys are not too deep and the rivers are not too wide. Kilkenny's mountains, the Walsh Mountains, in the south-west of the county, never rise higher than 313 metres while Mount Brandon, near Graiguenamanagh, is the highest peak, reaching 516 metres.

Kilkenny is built on the river Nore which takes its name from the Irish: *feoir* or *fér* meaning grass, because of its green grassy banks. The Nore, 140 km long, rises in County Tipperary, its sources flowing from the Slieve Bloom and Devils Bit mountains. It flows east through Borris, then turns south-easterly, passing through Durrow, Ballyragget, Kilkenny city, Bennetsbridge, Thomastown and Inistioge before joining the Barrow at New Ross, County Wexford.

A great limestone plain dominates the centre of the county with hills ringed around. This geological saucer-shape accounts for Kilkenny's very high temperatures in the summer and very cold temperatures in winter. The highest temperature ever recorded in Ireland (33.3 degrees Celsius) was registered in Kilkenny's Castle Park on 26th June, 1887. The plentiful supply of limestone, which paved the streets of Kilkenny in the 1700s, has given rise to Kilkenny's nickname, the Marble City. In 1750, William Colles devised a water-driven machine to cut and polish black marble which became the basis of an important industry at the Marble Works, Maddoxtown, a few miles outside Kilkenny.

Kilkenny is also known as Ye Faire Citie. This title may be attributed to the English poet Edmund Spenser who visited Kilkenny in 1580 and 1581, and wrote of,

'... the stubborn Newre whose waters gray
By faire Kilkenny and Rosseponte boord'

The adjective faire was soon used in relation to Kilkenny and the motto Ye Faire Citie was incorporated into Kilkenny's coat of arms which can be seen on the castle side of the Tholsel.

Kilkenny County and City take their name from the Irish *Cill Chainnigh,* meaning cell or church of Canice. Saint Canice was born in Derry in 514 AD. His father was a distinguished poet and his mother's name was Mella or Maul after whom the ancient church of Saint Maul's, once situated at the eastern end of Green's Bridge, was called. He died around 599 AD.

Saint Canice founded numerous churches in Scotland and Ireland and was known as 'Builder of Churches'. Whether or not he founded a church in Kilkenny is uncertain, but a church dedicated to Canice was established on a strategic knoll overlooking the fording point of the river Nore (which is the present day Green's Bridge). Saint Canice's Cathedral now occupies the site of this church of Canice and it was around this monastic settlement that the town of Kilkenny grew and evolved.

After the Anglo-Norman invasion of Kilkenny, Saint Canice's Cathedral became the centre of a separate borough called Irishtown. Kilkenny Castle became the centre of the other borough, called Englishtown or Hightown (which gave its name to High Street). Each borough returned Members of Parliament until the Act of Union in 1801 made them into a single constituency. Each borough also maintained separate corporations until their abolition in 1843.

Kilkenny was granted a town charter in 1208 by William the Earl Marshall. Its purpose was to attract immigrant workers and to create a thriving centre of trade as well as a military stronghold in Kilkenny.

In 1266, the Prince of Wales granted Kilkenny the 'Charter of Murage', an official document giving permission to a town or city to build fortifying walls. The charter was ratified by his father King Henry II. The presence of fortifying walls signified that this was a town of status and importance.

In 1400 Robert Talbot completed the stone walls of Kilkenny City, when he 'enclosed with walls the better part of the town by which it was greatly fortified'. Talbot's Tower, part of the old fortifying wall with its cobble-domed ceiling and five-foot thick walls, can still be seen in the grounds of Ormonde College (formerly the Vocational School) on Ormonde Road. A canon found in Talbot's Tower in 1854 is now in the National Museum. It is the only piece of artillery surviving from the city's defences. The wall was constructed from locally quarried limestone, mostly from the Black Quarry, it averaged 1.2 metres to 1.4 metres in thickness and survives to a height of 4.5 metres in places.

Kilkenny's wall had thirteen gates: Castle Gate, beside the Castle; St. Patrick's Gate, across from Butler House; Walkin's Gate, across from the Friary; St. James's Gate, near the James's St. entrance to Market Cross shopping centre; Black Freren Gate in Abbey St. (the only remaining gate); Irishtown Gate or the Watergate, across from the Watergate Theatre; Dean's Gate, near St. Canice's Catholic church; Troy's Gate, at the far end of Vicar St.; Green's Gate, near the city end of Green's Bridge; St. John's Outer Gate, at the junction of Michael St. and Maudlin St.; St. Magdalen's Gate, at the castle in Maudlin St. and St. John's Gate, on the Rose Inn St. side of John's Bridge.

THE STATUTE OF KILKENNY

Outside of Dublin, the Irish Parliament met most often in Kilkenny. In 1366 the Parliament of Kilkenny, under Lionel of Clarence, son of King Edward III, enacted the Statute of Kilkenny. The Statute, which was written in French, contained thirty six clauses dealing with administrative, legal, social and military problems faced by the Anglo-Normans in Ireland. The Statute was intended to prevent the Anglo-Normans becoming 'more Irish than the Irish themselves'.

Following are some conditions of the legislation:

Severe penalties shall befall those who:
  – Cut their hair in the Irish style
  – Speak in the Irish tongue
  – Play hurley or other games of the Irishry
  – Sell horses, armour or victuals to the Irish in time of war
  –Form alliances with the Irish whether by marriage, concubinage or fostering.

The Statute of Kilkenny was considered to be the most notorious piece of Irish legislation of the Middle Ages.

THE GOLDEN AGE

Kilkenny became a city by means of a charter of King James I of England, which was issued on 16th October, 1609. Nicholas Langton, who lived over the Butter Slip in High Street, accepted the charter on behalf of the city. Nicholas, who was twice married, had twenty-five children.

Kilkenny's 'Golden Age' lasted a little over a century, from about 1520 until 1650, during which time it enjoyed great commercial prosperity. Throughout this period Kilkenny was ruled by rich merchant families who, between them, controlled every office of church and state that Kilkenny had to offer. These family names were so well known that they have come down to us as a jingle:

Archdekin, Archer, Cowley, Langton, Lee
Knaresborough, Lawless, Raggett, Rothe and Shee.

It was these ten families who built the great stone houses that gave Kilkenny its reputation, and it was the politically astute members of these families who, in 1609, achieved city status for Kilkenny.

THE CONFEDERATION OF KILKENNY

In 1642 Kilkenny became the Provisional Capital of all Ireland. Leading Catholics, nobility and gentry, inspired by the Catholic uprising in Ulster and the civil war in England between Parliament under Oliver Cromwell, and King Charles I, convened in Kilkenny to set up a provisional government. Kilkenny being Ireland's largest inland town, with spacious housing and plentiful lodging, proved an appropriate meeting place.

Under the guidance of Dr. David Rothe (Catholic Bishop of Ossory), the General Assembly met in the house of Robert Shee, Coal Market (now Parliament Street). Shee's house was a substantial building with thirty three rooms; one of the rooms was spacious enough to hold the assembly and became known as Confederation Hall. Six members were elected from each province to form a Supreme Council and Kilkenny became the seat of the Confederate Parliament which sided with King Charles I.

For three years the government of Ireland was regulated by the Confederation of Kilkenny. Monies were minted, taxes levied and armies raised. In 1645 a new power was added to the Council. Cardinal Rinuccini, the Papal Nuncio, arrived in Kilkenny with £20,000 and arms for 6,000 men. He was greeted by thousands and paraded the length of the city.

While the Old English were happy to reach a settlement with King Charles, Rinuccini hoped for an outright victory for the Irish and a return of their lands. However, in 1649, King Charles I was executed. Cardinal Rinuccini returned to Rome, and one year later Cromwell arrived in Ireland. After a week-long siege, Kilkenny surrendered.

AFTER CROMWELL

Life in Ireland under Cromwell (1650 - 1658) was grim and joyless and it was no different in Kilkenny. The city has records of official Puritan orders forbidding bowls, playing cards, walking around town at church-time and gambling on tombstones. Between 1654 and 1657, two hundred of Kilkenny's leading citizens, men and women, were expelled from the city, and their properties confiscated by Cromwellian families.

Two years after Oliver Cromwell's death, King Charles II had his body dug up, sat the corpse in a chair and tried him for treason. Found guilty (of course), Charles had the corpse beheaded! Charles II tolerated the Catholic religion, and many of the Catholic families and priests, banished by Cromwell, returned to Kilkenny and were once again permitted to hold administrative positions.

Kilkenny, however, was never the same after its capture by Cromwell. The continued rise of Dublin and Waterford after 1660 meant that Kilkenny never had the same economic importance as before, and it was never again the political nerve centre that it had been during the short lived Confederation of Kilkenny.

Matters were not improved when the Catholic James II was beaten at the Battle of the Boyne in 1690 by William of Orange, who seized the throne of England. James had stayed in Kilkenny Castle and granted Kilkenny a university, the University of St. Canice, which was quickly abolished by King William.

The introduction of the Penal Laws, which excluded Catholics from government service, from the armed forces, from the legal profession, from attending mass and receiving further education, exacerbated Kilkenny's decline. Kilkenny, like much of Ireland, was now dominated by families, mostly of Cromwellian origin, who controlled most of the civic offices, and who resided in the Big House.

Agriculture, in particular cattle and grain, was the mainstay of Kilkenny's economy in the seventeenth and eighteenth centuries. Coal mining was also of great importance, the mines being situated in Castlecomer, 20 km north of the city. The construction of mills along the river Nore and the development of brewing further strengthened the economy. The woollen industry was the city's main source of employment throughout the eighteenth century, while flour was considered the 'true gold of Kilkenny' and the ultimate source of the finance that promoted the luxury trades of the city.

From the 1780s until the 1820s the social life of Kilkenny revolved around the annual theatre season. Visiting companies performed in the Tholsel, the Castle and the Courthouse (Grace's Castle). In 1802, the Kilkenny Players, gentlemen actors who raised monies for 'the charitable institutions of Kilkenny', founded their own theatre on the Parade, where Tom Moore, 'the bard of Ireland', performed. The Kilkenny theatre season was one of the highlights of the Irish social calendar with races during the day and balls and concerts in the evenings. It was said that mothers with marriageable daughters found Kilkenny second only to Bath, in England, for finding them suitable husbands.

THE NINETEENTH CENTURY TO THE PRESENT DAY

In 1831 Kilkenny city had a population of 23,741. By 1861 this had dropped to 14,000. The population decline was well under way before the Great Famine (1845–1849) struck. Due to the prompt action of the workhouse governors, very few people actually died in the city from starvation. At one stage the workhouse, built to accommodate 1,300 paupers, was home to over 4,000 people. The overcrowded conditions in the workhouse, however, spread disease, and by 1848 over

2,000 people had died. Kilkenny's population never recovered from the devastation of the famine and by 1901, aided by the city's lack of industrialisation and emigration, it had fallen to 10,000.

Kilkenny's failure to become highly industrialised was not without its advantage, as its beautiful stone buildings, old shop fronts and laneways remained unscathed by progress. Kilkenny also began to flourish culturally, with the foundation of literary and historical societies. The Archaeological Society, which was responsible for the preservation and restoration of many of Kilkenny's historic buildings (not least its own headquarters, Rothe House), was founded in 1849.

The Gaelic League *(Conradh na Gaeilge),* founded in 1893, and the Gaelic Athletic Association (GAA), founded in 1884, revived a nationwide interest in the Irish language, native games and Irish culture in general. This interest was spearheaded in Kilkenny by Standish O'Grady (1846–1928), barrister, historian and editor of the *Kilkenny Moderator,* who was recognised as the 'Father of the Irish Revival'. O'Grady was ably assisted by his friend Ottway Cuffe, the fifth Earl of Desart and his widowed sister-in-law Lady Ellen, Countess of Desart. Ottway Cuffe built the theatre in Patrick St. (now Zuni's restaurant), and as the twentieth century progressed,

Kilkenny began to establish itself as a city of heritage and culture.

The restoration of Kilkenny's heritage sites, the Castle, Rothe House, Shee Alms House and Kyteler's Inn, established Kilkenny as a major tourist destination and as the Medieval Capital of Ireland. The foundation of the Kilkenny Design Centre in 1963 attracted artists and craftspeople to the city, many of whom set up studios throughout the city and county. The locating of the Crafts Council of Ireland in Kilkenny in 1989 bolstered the creative ethos of the city and helped make Kilkenny the Crafts Capital of Ireland.

Kilkenny might equally be called the Festival Capital of Ireland. Back in 1963 the Kilkenny Beer Festival was launched. It ran for ten consecutive years and was one of the most popular festivals in the country, attracting tourists from all over the world. The main feature of the festival was the gigantic beer tent in James's park which seated 2,000 people, who were entertained by the Bavarian Brass Band, complete with lederhosen and traditional German costume.

In 1974 the Beer Festival was superseded by Kilkenny Arts Week, now the Kilkenny Arts Festival, which takes place in August. Featuring renowned international musicians, artists and writers, and incorporating theatre, street carnival and a host of fringe activities, it is one of Ireland's major cultural events.

The Rhythm & Roots Music Festival kicks off the May bank holiday weekend and has become one of the most popular events on the Irish music calendar. In June and July there's the Midsummer Music Festival in the beautiful open-air amphitheatre of Ballykeefe, near Kilmanagh. The internationally acclaimed Cat Laughs Comedy Festival runs throughout the June bank holiday weekend and features the cream of stand-up comedians from around the world.

In early October, Kilkenny hosts the Celtic Festival, which focuses on all things Celtic; song, dance, literature, arts & crafts, and it celebrates our rich Irish heritage and culture.

Other festivals in October include the Rockfall Music Festival, the Irish Conker Championship in Freshford, and the Gowran Park Horse Racing Festival.

The people of Kilkenny are known as the Kilkenny Cats. This nickname arose from the constant squabbling between Kilkenny's two corporations, one Irish and one English or Anglo-Norman, who viewed each other suspiciously across the dividing river Breagagh which can be seen beside the Watergate Theatre in Irishtown.

The corporation of Irishtown centred around the old Gaelic settlement of Saint Canice's Cathedral, while the corporation of Hightown or Englishtown centred around the new Norman settlement that was Kilkenny Castle. The squabbling went on until the two corporations were amalgamated in 1843.

A more colourful theory is that the nickname Kilkenny Cats originated with Cromwell's soldiers when they occupied the city in 1650. The story goes that the bored militiamen, for their amusement, were wont to tie two cats by their tails, throw them across a line and let them tear each other asunder.

One evening some soldiers were involved in the practice when they heard an officer coming; the sergeant responsible for the cat-fight slashed the cats down with his sword, leaving only their tails still tied to the line. "Have they eaten each other down to that?", the commanding officer inquired.

The following well-known rhyme probably originated from the Cromwellian cat story:

There once were two cats from Kilkenny
Each thought there was one cat too many
So they fought and they fit
They scratched and they bit

Till excepting their nails
And the tips of their tails
Instead of two cats there weren't any.

"Come on the cats!", the war-cry of Kilkenny hurling fans, can be heard to this day, not least when the Kilkenny team runs on to Croke Park, on the second Sunday in September, to contest yet another All Ireland Hurling Final.

Today Kilkenny is a vibrant, thriving city with a cosmopolitan atmosphere and a flourishing tourist industry. It's a city where crafts, cultural events and contemporary shopping blend quietly in the medieval ambience of its narrow laneways, slips and Norman Castle.

Saint Canice's Cathedral is the second longest medieval cathedral in Ireland after Saint Patrick's in Dublin. It is built on an old monastic settlement from which Kilkenny gets its name, *Cill Chainnig,* meaning church or cell of Canice. This early church was more than likely built by a follower of Saint Canice.

Hugh de Mapilton, Bishop from 1251–1260, has been named as 'the first founder of the Cathedral', the work being completed in 1285.

The round tower alongside the cathedral is the oldest part of the complex. Round towers were a feature of most Irish monasteries and were primarily used as bell towers. They were also, purportedly, used as watch towers, repositories for church valuables and places of refuge from invading marauders.

In 1650 Oliver Cromwell occupied Kilkenny and used Saint Canice's Cathedral to stable his horses. The magnificent stained glass window, which had been installed by Bishop Richard de Ledrede in 1354, and depicted 'the entire life, passion and resurrection of our Lord', was smashed. A few years earlier, during the Confederation of Kilkenny, Cardinal Rinuccini, the Papal Envoy, sought to buy the window for £700 and bring it to Rome. The offer was refused.

A flat shelf on the top of Saint Canice's tower is known as 'Cromwell's Seat' after Oliver Cromwell, who may well have observed the city from this vantage point.

Today, St. Canice's Cathedral holds services for the local Church of Ireland congregation. It also plays a prominent part in Kilkenny's Arts Festival, staging performances by internationally acclaimed orchestras and choirs.

Saint Canice's Cathedral

In 1172, the Anglo-Norman Richard Fitzgilbert de Clare (Strongbow) built a wooden fortification on the present site of Kilkenny Castle. Between 1192 and 1195, Strongbow's son-in-law, William Marshall, built a stone castle on this site.

Kilkenny Castle has become synonymous with the Butler family who came to Ireland with the Normans. Originally called Fitzwalter, they changed their name to Butler on acquiring the royal title of Chief Butler of Ireland, in 1185. This title required that they present the newly crowned King of England with the first goblet of wine. They also collected lucrative duty on all imported wines.

In 1391, James Butler, 3rd Earl of Ormonde, bought Kilkenny Castle from the Despenser family, William Marshall's heirs, for £800. The Butler dynasty would occupy the castle for over 500 years.

When King Edward VII visited the castle in 1904, he asked who the people lining up to meet him were. "They are the Butlers", came the reply. "Then why aren't they serving the bloody drinks then?", the monarch retorted.

The Castle was almost embroiled in the Civil War. The Marquess of Ormonde wrote: '

It was on the morning of the 2nd May, 1922 that, at the unreasonable hour of 5.30, I was awakened by a knock at the door. My butler appeared and greeted me with: "Excuse me disturbing your Lordship but the Republicans have taken the castle"' They were immediately besieged by the Free Staters but after a siege lasting several days the castle was restored to the Butlers'.

In 1935 the Butler family decided to leave Kilkenny Castle. A ten-day auction disposed of the contents, except for some tapestries and paintings, and the castle lay vacant for the next thirty two years. In 1967, Arthur Butler, 24th Earl of Ormonde, gave Kilkenny Castle to the people of Kilkenny for the nominal sum of £50. In an address he said:

"The people of Kilkenny, as well as myself and my family, feel a great pride in the Castle, and we have not liked to see this deterioration. We determined that it should not be allowed fall into ruins. There are already too many ruins in Ireland".

In 1969 the Long Gallery and north wing were refurbished. In 1994 the central interiors were restored in the style of an 1830s country house, and in 2000, the Parade Tower wing was developed as a purpose built conference and cultural centre.

Kilkenny Castle

A. Phelan '07

Kilkenny Castle, like any castle, boasts many colourful tales involving knights-in-armour, earls, princes and kings. But perhaps the most unusual and most daring of all those tales is that of a simple love story between two women; a love story that defied the customs and traditions, moral and otherwise, of the time.

The story of the Ladies of Llangollen, as they became known, is rather unique in the context of 18th century Ireland. Lady Eleanor Butler, daughter of the 16th Earl of Ormonde, was born in 1739. Educated in France, she was a very bright student with an independent mind, which made her a rather difficult and rebellious daughter. As it happened little love was lost between Lady Eleanor and her family.

When she was thirty Eleanor met Sarah Ponsonby, a shy, sensitive fourteen year old school girl. Sarah was an orphan who lived with her relations, the Fownes, at Woodstock House in Inistioge, County Kilkenny. Lady Eleanor and Sarah became very attached. Eleanor more or less educated the enthusiastic Sarah and they continued to correspond after Sarah had grown up.

Sir William Fownes, Sarah's guardian was very attracted to his ward and attempted to seduce her but Sarah rejected his advances. Like Sarah in Woodstock House, Lady Eleanor in Kilkenny Castle was equally unhappy and frustrated. In March 1778, Lady Eleanor and Sarah absconded to Waterford. Their families were scandalised by what they considered to be an unnatural relationship.

Two days later they were brought back. Lady Eleanor was sent to stay with relatives and placed under house arrest. Three weeks later Eleanor escaped to Woodstock House where she was concealed in a cupboard in Sarah's room. This time the families reluctantly agreed to their leaving and made a meagre financial arrangement for their future.

Lady Eleanor and Sarah spent the rest of their lives in a cottage in Llangollen in Wales, *'devoting their hearts and minds to self-improvement, to eschewing the vanities of society and to better, in so far as they could, the lot of the poor and the unfortunate'.*

Lady Eleanor Butler died in 1829, aged 92 years. Sarah Ponsonby, sixteen years her younger, died two years later.

The Ladies of Llangollen

KILKENNY CASTLE

20

K. Phelan'01

The Black Abbey, the official title of which is Abbey of the Most Holy Trinity, was 267 years old when Christopher Columbus discovered America. It was founded in 1225 AD by William Marshall, the younger Earl of Pembroke. The Black Abbey gets its name from the black cappa or cape that the Dominicans wore over their white habits, and it is the only Dominican foundation in Ireland to have survived on its original site.

In 1543, during the Reformation, King Henry VIII confiscated the Black Abbey. The community was dispersed and the church was turned into a courthouse. Sixty years later, however, the people of Kilkenny seized it and returned it to the Dominicans.

In 1650 the abbey was sacked by Cromwell's forces to such an extent that only the tower and parts of the walls remained standing. The Black Abbey was reopened for public worship in 1816 and was completely restored in 1979. The great stained-glass window, known as the Rosary Window because it depicts the Joyful, Sorrowful and Glorious mysteries of the rosary, is the largest of its kind in Ireland.

Prior to Kilkenny's flood relief scheme, the Black Abbey was particularly susceptible to flooding from the nearby river Breagagh (meaning 'false' from the Irish). The river was aptly christened, as in summer it would practically vanish underground, while in winter it occasionally wreaked havoc on the residents of Irishtown and the community of the Black Abbey.

During the great flood of 1947, the waters are said to have reached as high as 4.6 metres (15 feet). As they rose rapidly to the level of the main altar, Fr. Henry Gaffney, a member of the Dominican community, plunged into the rising flood to rescue the host and sacred vessels in the tabernacle.

Just across from the Black Abbey is the last remaining gate of the medieval wall that once surrounded and protected Kilkenny: Black Freren Gate, named after the black-caped friars of the abbey. The Black Abbey is still home to the Dominican order and is very much in use to this day.

The Black Abbey

A. Phelan 06

The Tholsel, in High Street, gets its name from two old English words: 'tol' meaning tax and 'sael' meaning a hall. Tholsels were common to all Norman towns and were essentially places where taxes were paid. Down the years, Kilkenny's Tholsel has had several functions; it was the guildhall and meeting place for merchants, a customhouse and a courthouse. Plays, light-operas and operettas were also performed there. The covered arcade of the Tholsel was common to many of the houses running along High Street.

There have been three Tholsels in Kilkenny. The first was built on the site of the Allied Irish Bank in High Street in the 14th century. The second was built on the site of the present Tholsel and was erected in 1575. The present Tholsel was erected in 1761 at a cost of £1,315 and was restored in 1949 for £49,000. On 20th September, 1985 it was gutted by fire and required major restoration work. It reopened on 1st February, 1987.

Some of the city's most important documents are stored in the Tholsel. Kilkenny has been more fortunate than any other town in Ireland, save Dublin, in the number and importance of its early records. Among these documents is the *Liber Primus Kilkenniensis* (the First Book of Kilkenny) which is Kilkenny's oldest book, containing city records from 1231 to 1537. The *Liber Primus* is printed on vellum and bound in oak.

Another very special document is the famous 1609 Charter from King James I of England granting city status to Kilkenny. These documents were originally kept in a chest which had three locks for security reasons. Three keys were required to open the locks; the City Sovereign held one, the City Recorder held another while the High Sheriff held the third. As tight as the security was, however, the *Liber Secundus Kilkenniensis* (the Second Book of Kilkenny) containing records from 1516 to 1544 went missing and has yet to be located (we live in hope!).

The city's archives are still housed in the Tholsel (in a safe), and many of them have been reproduced in a splendid book, the brainchild of former Mayor, Mrs. Betty Manning, called *Treasures of Kilkenny*, with text by John Bradley and photographs by Tom Brett.

Today the Tholsel, or City Hall, is home to Kilkenny's local government offices and the Borough Council meets there.

The Tholsel

A. Phelan '06

Rothe House, in Parliament Street, is a Tudor Merchant's House and is the finest of its kind to survive in Ireland. It was built by John Rothe Fitz Piers and his wife, Rose Archer, in 1594, when William Shakespeare was 30 years old. There were many such houses in Kilkenny in the 16th century, notably those of the leading civic families, the most prominent of whom were the Archers, Rothes and Shees.

The Rothes had twelve children and built on two more houses to the rear of Rothe House. Because of their close involvement with the Confederation of Kilkenny (1642–1649) the Rothe family suffered greatly under Cromwell. In 1653, John Rothe's son Peter was ordered to Connaught with his entire household. The Rothes lost everything after the Battle of the Boyne in 1690 and left Ireland with other Irish nobles in what became known as the 'Flight of the Wild Geese'. They later distinguished themselves on the battlefields of Europe.

Rothe House was used as a school in the 19th century. John and Michael Banim, the Kilkenny novelists, attended around 1808 and penned a fine description of the schoolmaster and the house. The Gaelic league, a nationwide movement to promote the revival of the Irish language, set up in the house in 1900 and Thomas McDonagh, one of the signatories of the 1916 Proclamation and a professor in St. Kieran's College, taught Irish there.

Part of Rothe House was bought by Kilkenny Archaeological society in 1962 and restored by the Office of Public Works. In 1980 the Society became sole owners of the entire complex, consisting of three houses separated by two courtyards. The third house was restored and officially opened by former President Mary Robinson in 1995. New Building Lane, just beside Rothe House, gets its name from the third house of Rothe House, which was always referred to as the New Building. Work is presently afoot to re-create the garden to the rear of the third house.

Rothe House today features a book shop, a library, a genealogical service and a museum where, among numerous historical documents and artefacts, is the key which Eamon De Valera, the former president of Ireland, used to escape from Lincoln Jail, in England, in 1919.

Rothe House

Shee Alms House, Kilkenny's Tourist Office, in Rose Inn Street is one of the few surviving Tudor Alms houses in Ireland. It was built in 1582 by Sir Richard Shee, a brilliant lawyer, to accommodate twelve paupers: six men and six women.

Richard Shee held the office of Deputy Treasurer of Ireland and was knighted in 1582. Extremely wealthy, he was also very religious and his founding of the Alms House may well have been an attempt to give back to the people of Kilkenny some of that wealth. He may also have considered it his insurance policy for the hereafter.. He gave money to the inmates every week to purchase their own food, fuel and clothing. He provided medical attention when they were ill, and when they died Sir Richard buried them at his own expense.

Shee Alms House survived as a charitable institution for three centuries – an extraordinary length of time – although Richard Shee's will stated that the house should continue for all time.

The longevity of the charity was undoubtedly aided by the reference in Shee's will to his *curse which will descend on any of his family who neglects his Alms House*.

The Penal Laws (discriminatory laws against Catholics) took their toll on the Shee family and in 1752 the house was sold by Edmund Shee. The inmates were not evicted but they had to depend on the generosity of the citizens of Kilkenny to survive. The Shee family regained ownership of the house in 1756, and the last record of any inmates being in the house is 1830.

During the Penal Days, Catholic Priests on the run from the forces of the Crown, frequently celebrated mass in Shee Alms House while worshippers knelt among the tombstones in nearby St. Mary's graveyard. Relations between Catholics and Protestants were so good that when mass was being celebrated, the Protestants kept watch in case the authorities might arrive and arrest the priest.

In 1912 Shee Alms House was leased as a store which finally brought to an end the long tradition of the Alms House as a charitable institution.

Shee Alms House was restored to its original condition in 1978 and in 1981 it was reopened as Kilkenny's Tourist Office.

Shee Alms House

Grace's Castle (or Grace's Oldcastle), better known as the Court House, was originally the site of the town house or castle of the influential Anglo Norman Grace family. Situated in Parliament Street – once known as Coal Market because coal was brought from Castlecomer and sold there – it was built in 1210 by William le Gros or William Grace.

The Grace family 'became more Irish than the Irish themselves' and in1566 James Grace donated the building, then known as Grace's Castle, to the townspeople for use as a county jail. In return, he was appointed Chief Constable or Governor of the jail, and given an annual income of £6 13s 4d for life. The castle was converted into a courthouse sometime between 1758 and 1794, when the first recorded sitting of the Assize Court took place there.

For almost a quarter of a century, from approximately 1767 to 1792, the County Courthouse was Kilkenny's chief theatrical venue, and was transformed over and over again to suit the various productions presented there. It was billed as Theatre Royal by the 'Strollers', professional actors from Dublin, and Private Theatre by 'The Gentlemen Players', Kilkenny gentlemen who performed plays as fund-raisers for various charities.

Mr. Thomas Ryder, a veteran actor turned manager, brought his company to play at the County Courthouse in Coal Market in 1767. He was the first to turn the 'assizes hall' into 'a regular little theatre'. In 1768, his company staged Shakespeare's *Henry VIII*, *The Tempest* and a musical entitled *A Ramble Through Dublin* (amongst other productions).

During the 1798 rebellion, many of the Irish insurgents were executed outside the courthouse. For over 200 years this building has been a courthouse and still retains the features of a prison, the cells of which are still visible at street level. The cells, six feet by four feet, had one barred window, a wooden bed with straw, and could hold up to four prisoners. The stairs and balcony, where many a Kilkenny hurler held aloft the Liam McCarthy Cup on home-coming night, were added around 1830.

The Courthouse, or Grace's Castle, is still the seat of law in the city, and Kilkenny's District Court sits there to the present day.

Grace's Castle

The story of Alice Kyteler, Kilkenny's 'witch', is as colourful as any novel or movie. It's a story of intrigue, money, murder, power and strange nocturnal practices.

Alice Kyteler was anything but a toothless old hag in black cape and pointed hat. She lived in Kyteler's Hall, now Kyteler's Inn in Kieran Street, and was an intelligent, attractive and very resourceful woman.

Alice Kyteler had four husbands, three of whom died in mysterious circumstances, leaving her extremely wealthy and a powerful influence in the community. In 1324, her fourth husband Sir John le Poer, was *'reduced to such a state by powders, pills and potions, that he was totally emaciated, deprived of his nails, and his hair fell out'* (classic symptoms of arsenic poisoning).

In that same year, her stepchildren, alarmed at the high mortality rate of their fathers, and indignant at the ease with which Alice had relieved them of their inheritances, complained to the Bishop of Ossory, Richard de Ledrede, alleging that by sorceries and witchcraft, Alice had killed their fathers and induced them to give all their money to herself and her natural son William Outlawe.

Bishop de Ledrede, a Franciscan from London, set about charging Alice and 'a band of heretical sorcerers' with witchcraft.

One of the many charges went as follows:

'…in order to inflict death or disease on the body…they made powders and ointments containing certain horrible worms, curious herbs and dead men's nails which they cooked, with various incantations, in a vessel made from the skull of a decapitated thief.'

Alice, however, turned the tables on the Bishop, and with the aid of her influential friends (the Lord Chancellor of Ireland was her brother-in-law), had Bishop de Ledrede imprisoned in Kilkenny Castle for seventeen days.

On his release Bishop de Ledrede pressed ahead with his charges, forcing a confession from Alice's son William Outlawe. It seemed the game was up for Dame Alice but not quite! The night before her trial, Alice Kyteler, thanks yet again to her influential friends, slipped quietly out of the country, and was never heard of again. Bishop de Ledrede found a scapegoat in Petronella, Alice Kyteler's lady-in-waiting, who after many beatings and threats of eternal damnation, publicly confessed to sorcery and witchcraft. She was burned at the stake before a large crowd in High Street – the first ever burning of a 'witch' in Ireland.

Kilkenny's Witch

KYTELERS INN

A. Phelan 06

The original town of Kilkenny was based along a single main street, High Street. Two streets, Walkin Street and James Street, ran perpendicularly from it, and a backstreet, Low Lane, later known as King St. and now Kieran Street, ran diagonally from it. High Street is broader in the middle than at either ends and this deliberate design was to accommodate a row of stalls on market day.

The Parade was created by James Butler, the first Duke of Ormonde (1610–1688), who demolished the east side of Castle Street, now the Castle Road, to create a space in front of the castle where his soldiers could parade.

Parliament Street was formerly known as Coal Market, as coal was brought here from the Castlecomer mines to be sold. The name Parliament Street comes from the Confederation of Kilkenny, when the Parliament of all Ireland met at the house of Robert Shee in Coal Market. A plaque on the Bank of Ireland marks the site of Shee's house and commemorates the Confederation of Kilkenny.

The Butter Slip, the narrow lane-way beside the Tholsel, leading from High Street to Kieran Street, is so called because local women came here to sell butter. The Hole in the Wall Market was based in the Butter Slip and is celebrated in rhyme:

If ever you go to Kilkenny
Enquire for The Hole in the Wall

Where you get twenty four eggs for a penny
And butter for nothing at all

The Market Slip, at the other end of High Street, connects to Kieran Street also, and is so called because it led to the markets, which were traditionally held around the Market Yard area. In 1999, Kilkenny acquired a new street: Ormonde Street. The old Mahon & McPhillips offices and lands were acquired by the local authority, and after extensive urban development, Ormonde Street, which connects Patrick Street and New Street, was created.

Kilkenny's newest street, Haughney Green, off Gaol Road, was opened on 21st April, 2007. Haughney Green is unusual in that the housing development, comprising fourteen homes and a day centre for the elderly, was built by St. Mary's Voluntary Housing Association. Environment minister Dick Roche performed the opening, while Bishops Laurence Forristal and Michael Burrows gave the street an ecumenical blessing.

Some streets & slips

THE MARKET SLIP AND THE BUTTER SLIP

In the old days, travellers, rich and poor, were fed and sheltered free of charge in the abbeys and monasteries. When numbers became too great to cater for, inns were established close to the monasteries where the travellers were entertained without payment. These inns often had the sign 'Bull' outside. The word 'Bull' in this case had nothing to do with the animal but comes from the Latin *bulla* meaning seal, indicating that the inn was licensed under the seal of the abbey or monastery.

The Bull Inn, which was very close to St. Francis Abbey, was such a house of hospitality, attached to the abbey. It gave its name to the street where it stood, known as Bull Alley up to 1883 when it was widened and its name was changed to St. Canice's Place. Prior to its widening, Bull Alley was so narrow that people could almost shake hands across its roadway.

The Sheaf had the reputation of being the best inn in Ireland. It stood in Rose Inn Street, facing the Parade and sported a large, gilded representation of a sheaf of wheat over the door. The pub is now run by the Henderson family.

Other inns that have long vanished include The Munster Arms and The Brazen Head, both situated in Walkin Street. The Swan Inn was situated in William Street, then known as Bolton Lane, while The Kings Arms and The Red Lion were in John Street. The Bush Inn (now Syd Harkin's) and The Garter were in Rose Inn Street and The Goat's Beard and The Smulkin Tavern were on the Castle Road, then known as Castle Street. The George Inn was in Irishtown, while The Eagle Inn stood in Coal Market, now Parliament Street.

There is no shortage of 'inns' or 'taverns' in Kilkenny today. Indeed two of the city's finest hostelries can boast of being the best in Ireland. In 1977 Tynans Bridge House, on John's Bridge, won the Black & White Scotch Whisky 'Pub of the Year' inaugural award, while Langtons in John Street won it three times in a row, in 1988, 1989 and 1990, and just for good measure, they won it again in 1992.

Inns & Taverns
of Kilkenny

The Club House Hotel is the oldest hotel in Kilkenny. It was also the first establishment of its kind in the city to take the name of 'hotel' in place of the old term 'inn'. The Club House gets its name from the Kilkenny Foxhunters' Club, which was established in 1797 by Sir John Power. This club had its club house in Patrick Street, under the management of a Mr. Rice. In 1817, to exploit the opening of the new Cork road, it was formed into a hotel. Apart from catering for weary travellers, the hotel provided accommodation and sustenance for hunt members who were too exhausted (or not exhausted enough) to go home

John Walsh then entered into partnership with Mr. Rice. They added to the Club House the adjoining premises which had been the residence of Archdeacon Helsham. Messrs. Walsh and Rice opened this establishment on 4th August, 1817, calling it The Hibernian Hotel and Foxhunting Club. The excellent management and fare of the hotel became known far and near. In 1834, Henry Inglis, on a tour of Ireland, wrote of the Club House:

'The Club House or Hibernian Hotel, Kilkenny is one of the very best I have ever found in any country, London not excepted. The wine is better quality than in England and an excellent whiskey punch was to be had for five pence'.

Around the year 1859 a Mr. Simon Morris succeeded Messrs. Rice and Walsh as proprietor of the hotel. Mr. Morris often told of the great feat performed by Jack Courtenay, from County Cork, who for a wager of £50, rode his famous hunter *White Lion* from the Club House stables, up the hotel stairs into the club room, jumped a fire screen and rode back again to the stables. Mr. Courtenay was over sixty years of age at the time. He won the wager.

Mr. Thomas F. Murphy purchased the hotel in 1888. He renovated the premises, employing highly skilled Kilkenny craftsmen, and reopened it in 1889. The hotel continued to flourish until Mr. Murphy's death in 1922, after which his widow Mary ran the hotel. Mrs. Florence Lee subsequently took over the hotel and sold it to Jim Brennan in 1977. The Club House Hotel is still a popular meeting place for numerous clubs and societies, and is run by father and son team, Jim and Ian Brennan.

The Club House Hotel

A. Phelan '07

From the 1780s to the early 1800s, Kilkenny's most noted supper house was The Hole in the Wall, situated in the rear of the laneway opposite Mary's Lane, and not to be confused with that in the Butter Slip. This back street tavern (part of the Archer mansion built in 1582) was the most fashionable resort in the city. Arthur Wellesley, The Duke of Wellington and Prime Minister of Britain, remembered his suppers there: *'there was no drunkenness, just good fellowship and conversation to early in the morning'*. The origin of the name is unclear, though entrance to the tavern, from High St., may have been through 'a hole in the wall'.

The Hole in the Wall tavern is celebrated in the famous rhyme:

If ever you go to Kilkenny
Remember the Hole in The Wall
You get blind drunk there for a penny
And tipsy for nothing at all.

The Hole in the Wall was renowned, not just for its suppers, but for its breakfasts. A party of fifteen men ordered breakfast there on one occasion and the following verses ensued:

And quick two waiters bless our eyes
With two tureens of monstrous size
Which also vanished, quick as thought
For breakfast.

The pot of tripe I ordered bring
Tripe is a most delicious thing
Whatever else you have fetch in
For breakfast.

Then straight at his command were brought
Two platters large with tripe 'oerwrought
Which also vanished, quick as though
For breakfast.

Mutton, kidneys the board supplies
A turkey, cold, of pretty size
Six dozen eggs salute our eyes
For breakfast.

Numberless plates of toast were spread
From foot of table to the head
With prints of butter, loaves of bread
For breakfast.

The Hole in the Wall is now owned by Michael Conway, Consultant Cardiologist in St. Luke's hospital, Kilkenny, who is working on a sympathetic restoration.

The Hole in the Wall

FROM A 1926 SKETCH IN 'KILKENNY' BY SPARKS AND BLIGH

A. Phelan'07

The oldest brewery in Ireland is Saint Francis Abbey Brewery which stands on the site of a Franciscan Abbey founded in 1234 AD by Richard Marshall. A special feature of the church was the high altar, made from Kilkenny marble, which was one of the largest and most beautiful of its kind in Ireland. The diarist, Friar John Clyn, was a member of this community until his demise during the Black Death in 1349.

Brewing was carried on for centuries by the monks of the abbey until the dissolution of the monasteries around 1540. The building fell into disrepair but was subsequently restored and used for Catholic worship until the arrival of Cromwell in 1650 when his soldiers plundered the abbey. The ruins of St. Francis Abbey survive to this day in the grounds of Smithwick's Brewery, which was founded in 1710 by John Smithwick.

The Smithwick family came from Hertfordshire in England, and settled in Wexford before moving to Kilkenny. In the 1850s,

eight types of ale, stout and porter were on sale from the brewery. By 1873 Smithwick's had become the largest Irish brewery outside of Dublin and Cork. An eight-week strike in 1920 forced the end of stout and porter brewing. Smithwick's now brew three main ales: a cask ale, on draught, a premium ale 'No 1' and a strong, winter ale known as 'Barley Wine'.

In June 1964 the brewery was taken over by the Guinness Company. In 1966 it launched Smithwick's Draught Ale, which became an instant success and is still regarded by many (author included) as Ireland's favourite ale. In 1986 St. Francis Abbey Brewery started production of Budweiser, the world's best selling lager.

Kilkenny Beer, with its distinctive ruby red colour was originally developed for export. Launched in Germany in 1987, it is now available in over thirty countries throughout the world. Draught Kilkenny was launched in Ireland in July 1995.

St. Francis Abbey Brewery is now owned by Diageo. In 1997, Guinness and Grand Metropolitan, two giants of the drinks industry, merged to create Diageo, the largest wine and spirits business in the world. Diageo comes from the Latin for day and the Greek for world, the concept being that every day around the world, millions of people enjoy the company's brands.

Smithwick's Brewery

A. Phelan '06

Just outside of Kilkenny, on the road to Freshford, is a picturesque, traditional English-style village. This is Talbot's Inch, a cluster of houses, known in its day as a 'model village'. The appearance of an English 'model village' in Kilkenny is quite remarkable, and its existence is due to several factors.

Firstly, in the 19th century, wealthy English businessmen, influenced by their travels abroad, built 'model villages' such as Talbot's Inch, in German and Swiss styles, to accommodate their workers.

Secondly, the English Arts and Crafts Movement, pioneered by William Morris (1834–1896) promoting the value of handmade objects, prompted the Celtic Revival which sought to preserve Ireland's unique culture of art, crafts, music and games.

Around this time also, it became fashionable for absentee landlords to return to their Irish estates. One of these was Ottway Cuffe (1853–1912), the Fifth Earl of Desart, who returned to Kilkenny in 1899, after the premature death of his older brother William, the Fourth Earl of Desart, who had been married to Ellen Bischoffsheim (Lady Desart). A chance meeting with William Morris on a boat trip greatly influenced Ottway Cuffe, as did his friend Standish O'Grady, the editor of the *Kilkenny Moderator,* who stressed the importance of leadership from Anglo-Irish landlords.

It was Ottway Cuffe's vision, allied with the capital from his widowed sister-in-law Lady Desart that brought about the industrial 'model village' of Talbot's Inch, which was built in 1906. The distinctive low-eaved cottages with decorative brick patterns and thatched roofs, housed carpenters, painters, gardeners and artisans.

President of the Gaelic League, Ottway Cuffe, succeeded in his wish to make a worthwhile contribution to Kilkenny. At one stage, Talbot's Inch and the surrounding area hosted a woollen mill (Kilkenny Woollen Mills), a tobacco farm, a woodwork factory (Kilkenny Woodworkers Ltd), a hosiery factory, a dairy and a school. Lady Desart also built the best cottage hospital in the world - Aut Even (from the Irish, *áit aoibhinn,* meaning pleasant place), which is very much in use to this day.

Talbot's Inch, the traditional English 'model village' has changed considerably since the beginning of the 20th century. However, it is still visually unique and a rare link to a special time in Irish history.

Talbot's Inch

A. Phelan '07

Saint Mary's Cathedral, the seat of the Catholic Bishop of Ossory, is built on the site of Burrell's Hall, home of the first Diocesan College in Kikenny. Burrell was a Cromwellian favourite, who built the house on the high land known as the 'Windy Harbour'.

After 8 o'clock mass on the 18th August, 1843, the foundation stone of the new cathedral was laid by Right Rev. William Kinsella, Bishop of Ossory. A sealed bottle, containing Rules of the Society for Propagation of the Faith, Rules of the Christian Doctrine Society, a number of *Kilkenny Journals,* some silver coins and a metal plate commemorating the event, was placed in the foundation stone.

Kilkenny's new cathedral was modelled after Gloucester Cathedral. The architect was a Mr. Butler from Dublin and the material used was Kilkenny limestone. The tower of the cathedral is out of proportion to the nave. In the aftermath of the famine, finances were exhausted and the builders settled for five bays instead of the intended eight.

Fundraising commenced in 1842, and the subscribers, wealthy business people mostly, were from Saint Mary's parish only. The Bishop himself led off the proceedings with a donation of £100. Unfortunately, Bishop Kinsella, not yet 50 years of age, died in 1845, when the walls were only seven feet high. Dr. Edmond Walsh, the new bishop, inherited £6,000 fund money, and the remaining £19,000 was raised from private benefactors and by door to door collections. The fundraisers were called 'Honorary Collectors for St. Mary's Cathedral Building Fund', and once again the subscribers were parishioners of St. Mary's only.

Raising money was particularly difficult in 1845 when famine was devastating the country. The construction of the cathedral, however, created employment and gave the people a sense of purpose. The *Kilkenny Journal* of 1857 reported that *'as it rose, tier on tier of solid masonry, and began to take form before all eyes, the zeal and enthusiasm of the people knew no bounds'.*

On 30th September a notice appeared in the *Kilkenny Journal,* listing ticket prices for the grand opening. Prices ranged from: £1 single for the first division, 10 shillings for the second division, 5 shillings for the third division and for family tickets. The consecration of Saint Mary's Cathedral began at 6.15 am on Sunday morning, 4th October, 1857, and concluded around 9.00 am.

Saint Mary's Cathedral

The Kilkenny Design Centre is a unique showplace for the best of Irish and international craftsmanship. The Design Centre, as it's known locally, was once the stables of Kilkenny Castle. How the 18th century stables of Kilkenny Castle became the home of 21st century, contemporary design is the story of one man's vision for excellence.

Ireland of the early sixties was not very design-conscious. In an attempt to raise the standard of design in Irish industry, the Irish Export Board sought the advice of some eminent designers from Scandinavia, countries that had achieved exemplary export successes in textiles, furniture, ceramics and glass.

William Walsh, General Manager of the Irish Export Board, decided to convert the stables of Kilkenny Castle into an internationally recognised centre for design. In April 1963 the Kilkenny Design Workshops (KDW) came into existence. The 18th century stables were now home to designers and craft workers from Scandinavia, England, Scotland, Germany, Switzerland, USA and the Netherlands.

The renowned Irish artist Louis Le Brocquy designed the monogram KDW which identified products designed by the Kilkenny Design Workshops and which became its trademark. The restoration, by architect Niall Montgomery, was awarded the silver medal of the Royal Institute of Architects in Ireland and also received a National Heritage Award.

Mr. Walsh became chief executive of The Kilkenny Design Workshops and KDW quickly established a reputation for outstanding graphic, industrial and craft design. It subsequently opened shops in Dublin and in London. Many of the craft workers and designers established studios throughout the city and county, affirming Kilkenny as the 'Crafts Capital of Ireland'.

In 1989 KDW was privatised and the Castle Yard complex is now managed by Kilkenny Civic Trust. That same year, the Crafts Council of Ireland re-located to the city and is based in the crescent building of the complex, where Kilkenny Design Consultancy and a number of craft workers have studios.

Kilkenny Design Centre continues to show the best of Irish and international craft and design. The entrance building, with its arched gateway and copper-domed clock-tower, is now a landmark in Kilkenny city.

Kilkenny Design Centre

'A place of horror and vast solitude, a cave of robbers and a lair for those who lie in wait for blood.'

So wrote the Anglo-Norman Bishop of Ossory, Hugh de Rous, about Graiguenamanagh in the year 1204. A compliment, indeed, to the Gaels of Graigue who obviously resented the Norman invaders, who, despite their superior weaponry and armour, preferred to wait for the leaves to fall from the trees before venturing into the dense and dangerous woodland to subdue the native Celts.

It was these same Normans, however, who were responsible for the name Graiguenamanagh, the village of the monks, called after the Cistercian monks who came from the Abbey of Stanley in Wiltshire, at the invitation of William Marshall, Earl of Pembroke, to found Duiske Abbey in 1204.

The name Duiske comes from the Irish: *dubh uisce* meaning black water. The river Duiske, which rises in Mount Brandon gave Graiguenamanagh its pre-Norman, Gaelic name: *Bun Dubhuisce,* meaning the Lower Black Water.

Duiske Abbey became one of the first Gothic structures in Ireland, and one of the finest pieces of 'early English' architecture in the country. It was also the largest of the thirty-four medieval Cistercian monasteries in Ireland.

The Cistercian order was quite austere. As animal food was forbidden, the monks were all vegetarians. They wore neither linen nor furs, and because their habits were woven of undyed wool they were called *Mainigh Bán,* meaning the White Monks. They assembled for prayers seven times throughout the day and night.

The abbey prospered. Cattle and sheep were reared, wool was exported while a variety of crafts and trades were practised. With the dissolution of the monasteries in 1536, the community was scattered and Henry VIII rewarded James Butler, the 9th Earl of Ormonde, with the lands of the abbey for his loyalty to the Crown. The massacre of twelve monks in 1561 in the abbey heralded the end of the golden days of Duiske Abbey.

Mass, however, continued to be said there – even through the Penal times when the church was roofless and in ruins. Described as 'the church that refused to die', Duiske Abbey was completely renovated and re-opened in 1980 and is, once again, one of the most magnificent abbeys in Ireland. The abbey also hosts the annual Duiske concerts, featuring renowned Irish and international musicians.

Duiske Abbey, Graiguenamanagh

A. Phelan '07

Mention Gowran and most people will think of horse-racing or D.J. Carey, one of the greatest exponents of the game of hurling. Or both.

Gowran is, of course, the birth-place of D.J. Carey and it is also a very popular and picturesque venue for horse-racing. Gowran Racecourse held its inaugural meeting in 1914 and has been going strong ever since. Famous horses to kick their heels on the Gowran turf include *Arkle* and *Dawn Run*. Meetings are held almost every month; the main events being the Thyestes Chase in January, Glanbia Day in early May and the Kilkenny three-day Racing Festival in October.

Horse-racing and hurling aside, Gowran was a place of great strategic importance prior to the Norman invasion, as it commanded an ancient road through the surrounding marshlands. It was a royal residence for the Kings of Ossory, sometimes referred to as the 'Kings of Gowran'.

The medieval church of Saint Mary's was built in 1225. A tower was added in the 14th or 15th century and it now incorporates the ruins of a 19th century church. Some fine effigies and tombs can be seen here, including what may be the tombs of the 1st and 3rd Earls of Ormonde.

Theobald Fitzwalter, chief Butler of Ireland, under King Henry II of England, was allotted the lands of Gowran by Richard Fitzgilbert de Clare better known as Strongbow.

Gowran became the residence of the Butler family until they bought Kilkenny Castle in 1391.

James Butler, the 3rd Earl of Ormonde, built Gowran Castle in 1385 close to the site of the present castle while town walls were erected around the year 1415. Cromwell besieged the castle in 1650. Colonel Hammond and his officers surrendered and were shot; the chaplain, a Franciscan friar named Fr. Hilary Conroy, was hanged. A Magdalen hospital was built outside the town walls around 1578 'for the relief of poor leprous people'. In 1608, King James 1 made Gowran a Parliamentary Borough.

King William of Orange, fresh from his victory at the Battle of the Boyne, rode through Gowran in 1690 on his way to Kilkenny to stay with the Duke of Ormonde.

Charles Stewart Parnell, 'the Uncrowned King of Ireland', addressed a huge gathering on the Green in Gowran in 1890, a year before his death from pneumonia.

Gowran

ST. MARY'S CHURCH, GOWRAN

A. Phelan '07

Thomastown was founded at the beginning of the 13th century by the Anglo-Norman, Thomas Fitzanthony after whom the town is called; the English from his first name, Thomas, and the Irish, *Baile Mhic Andáin* from his surname. Thomastown was once a walled town with no less than fourteen castles but only a few ruins remain today.

Thomastown boasts many historical sights. Foremost among these is the 12th century Jerpoint Abbey, 2 km out the Waterford Road. Jerpoint is one of the finest Cistercian ruins in Ireland and its importance was such that, in medieval times, the town of Newtown-Jerpoint, which was mysteriously abandoned in the 17th century, evolved around it. The abbey is unique in having the most decorative cloister arcade of any Irish church, bearing a number of carved figures, detailing the clothing and armour worn in 15th and 16th century Ireland.

Just south of the town, the ruin of Grennan Castle, built by Thomas Fitzanthony, stands by the river Nore while 2.5 km away,

Dysart Castle, once home to Bishop Berkeley, Ireland's greatest philosopher, can be seen. A short drive out the Dublin road is Kilfane church where the effigy of a Norman knight, Thomas de Cantwell, known as Cantwell Fada or Long Cantwell, stands in full coat of chain mail with sword and shield.

The river Nore was the mainstay of the town for centuries, providing fishing, milling, trading and agriculture. Thomastown was foremost a milling town with as many as twelve water-powered mills working in its heyday. The arrival of the railway in the 19th century reduced the significance of the town as a trading point.

Thomastown today is vibrant, prosperous and home to two third-level craft schools: Grennan Mill Craft School and the Pottery Skills Course under the direction of the Crafts Council of Ireland. The church of St. Mary's, built in the 13th century, with a 'new' early 19th century church built within its ruin, stands at the top of Market Street.

Thomastown is synonymous with Mount Juliet, or Walton's Grove as it was known, built in the middle of the 18th century by the 1st Earl of Carrick. The McCalmont family purchased it in 1914 and sold it in 1987. It is now a luxury hotel with an internationally renowned golf-course, designed by Jack Nicklaus, which hosted the Irish Open in 1993, 1994 and 1995.

Thomastown

ST. MARY'S CHURCH, THOMASTOWN

A. Phelan '06

Santa Claus is buried in a little country graveyard in south Kilkenny! Incredible as this might seem there is evidence to substantiate the possibility that Saint Nicholas of Myra, the original Santa Claus, is actually buried just west of Jerpoint Abbey in County Kilkenny. The unmarked grave is said to be in the ruined church at Newtown-Jerpoint, 2km outside Thomastown, once the site of a thriving Norman town that was mysteriously abandoned in the 17th century.

Owen O'Kelly, in his book *A History of Kilkenny* (1969) wrote:

'… the ruined church and tower stand high and are well worthy of preservation. St. Nicholas's tomb with effigy in clerical garb is in the churchyard'.

St. Nicholas, Archbishop of Myra in Turkey, died in 342 AD, and was buried there. How the remains of St. Nicholas arrived in south Kilkenny has much to do with the Normans.

Jerpoint Abbey was founded in 1160, probably by Donal MacGillapatrick, King of Ossory. In 1180, it was taken over by the Cistercian order. In 1200, William Pembroke, Earl Marshall of Kilkenny Castle, decided to build a new town just across the river from Jerpoint Abbey. He called the town Nova Villa Juxta Geripons meaning 'The New Town Across from Jerpoint'. That same year the Church of St. Nicholas of Myra was built in the town and according to the historian Canon Carrigan, the tomb was laid that same year also.

When Strongbow invaded Ireland in 1169, his most trusted lieutenant was Sir Humphrey De Fraine. When the church of Newtown-Jerpoint was built and dedicated to St. Nicholas in 1200, the most powerful Anglo-Norman baron in south Kilkenny was Nicholas De Fraine, son of Sir Humphrey. The story goes that the Norman Knights of Jerpoint, the crusading De Freynes, when forced to evacuate the Holy Land, exhumed the remains of St. Nicholas of Myra and brought them to Normandy from where they eventually found their way to Jerpoint. The remains were laid to rest beneath a slab, now broken across the centre, depicting a monk in habit and cowl.

The grave, whether it be the real Santa Claus or not, can still be seen to this day.

Santa Claus and Jerpoint

A. Phelan '07

The name Kells comes from the Irish *Ceanannus* meaning the 'head seat' or 'residence'. According to the *Annals of the Four Masters* the name Ceanannus was given to any place where Fiacha Finnailches, one of the ancient high kings of Ireland, set up a residence.

There is archaeological evidence to suggest that the motte of Kells, an enlarged mound of stones behind the Catholic church, was the site of an ancient fortress before the arrival of the Normans. The motte, a natural defensive position, is believed by some historians to have been the principal seat of the kings of the ancient Irish kingdom of Ossory.

Kells Priory was founded in 1193 by the area's first Norman ruler, Geoffrey FitzRobert de Marisco. Its most striking feature is the series of medieval towers spaced at intervals along the walls, which enclose a site of over three acres. These give the priory the appearance of a fortress more so than a place of worship, which explains its local name 'the Seven Castles'.

The fortress appearance is understandable considering that the priory was sacked on several occasions. In 1252 it was sacked by the army of Lord William de Bermingham. Lord Edward Bruce took possession of the town in 1316, then eleven years later, in 1327, the town and priory were sacked and burned by Maurice Fitzgerald, Earl of Desmond.

The Augustinian canons of Kells Priory were not monks and did not live as an enclosed community. They were worldly and met with the laity far more than monkish orders. The priory generated a great deal of industry and incorporated a mill and a brewery.

Suppressed by Henry VIII around 1540, the priory and much of its lands were granted to James Butler, 9th Earl of Ormonde. With the arrival of Cromwell in 1590, the Priory dissipated further and the once thriving medieval settlement went into permanent decline.

The present ruin is one of the largest and most complete in Ireland and during the Kilkenny Arts Festival exhibits sculpture by renowned Irish and international artists.

Just beside the Protestant Church is Boithrín na gCorp, meaning 'laneway of the bodies' in Irish. Boithrín na gCorp takes its name from the funeral processions to the churchyard.

Kells and its Priory

Two family names are very much associated with Castlecomer – the O'Brennans from Idough and the Wandesfordes from Yorkshire. In 1614 the O'Brennans surrendered their lands to Black Tom, the 10th Earl of Ormonde, and in 1636 those lands were granted to Sir Christopher Wandesforde who designed and built the town.

It was Sir Christopher who developed the local anthracite mines with which Comer will always be associated. In 1640 the first seam opened by him was called 'The Old Three Foot'. In 1875 it was estimated that 'The Old Three Foot' had produced as much as 15 million tons of coal – a phenomenal amount for such a small seam.

Because the seams were not as deep as the coalfields of Britain, it was common practice for a Castlecomer miner to work on his side 'colliering' or 'digging out with a pick', on a coalface only eighteen inches high. On a positive note, it was possible to use naked lights in the mines as anthracite doesn't contain methane gas and so fatalities were less common.

In 1924 a shaft was sunk in Castlecomer's Deerpark site which became known as the 'Deerpark Pit'. The coal proved to be comparable with the best anthracite found anywhere in the world. Between 1930 and 1960, the Deerpark mine employed around 400 to 550 men underground and 150 on the surface. Although companionship in the pithead was good, mining was a difficult life and there was much hardship and suffering.

In 1932 a bitter strike started, spearheaded by Nixie Boran and brothers, Jimmy and Tommy Walsh, to improve the working and living conditions of the Castlecomer miners. Because of their socialist leanings, these three, along with many others, found themselves fighting mine-owners, church and state, a battle that they inevitably lost but not without gaining some advancement for the miners and much respect and admiration for their integrity and resilience.

At 4 pm on 31st January 1969, the Deerpark mine closed after forty five years in operation, bringing to a close the three hundred and twenty nine year history of mining in Castlecomer.

On a lighter note, Castlecomer is now renowned for its famous Wellie Race held every New Years Day, which raises thousands of Euros for local charities.

Castlecomer

THE AVALON INN, CASTLECOMER

The history of Kilkenny is more or less the story of the Norman invaders conquering the native Celts. Nice then to see Kilkenny do a little 'conkering' of its own for a change.

The 'conkering' in question involves the age-old game of conkers, whereby two people, 'armed' with a chestnut on a string, take alternate swings at each other's conker until such time as one breaks or disintegrates. The 'conkering' takes place in the village of Freshford in County Kilkenny and the event is the Irish Conker Championship – the only conker event of its kind in the country.

For several years now Freshford has been staging the Irish Conker Championship which takes place on the last Sunday in October. The history of the conker championship goes back to the year 2000 when the Freshford Heritage and Development Committee inaugurated the National Conker Championship to coincide with the creation of a local Millennium Park.

Inspiration came from the fact that Freshford's village square contains 52 horse chestnut trees, one for every week of the year, which were planted by the Eyre family in 1911. That inaugural Conker Festival was a tremendous success and it has now become an annual event.

In 2002 Ireland's Conker team, comprising Grace Kearney, Liam Barnaville, Joe Dermody and Eamon Dooley, all from Freshford, travelled to Ashton in England to participate in the World Conker Championship. Participants from twenty countries descended on the tiny hamlet in Hampshire to try and become the 'Conker Champion of the World'.

Eamon Dooley surpassed himself by breaking a phenomenal 306 conkers in the space of one hour. This achievement merited him a coveted place in the *Guinness Book of Records*, the first ever entry for this unusual 'sport'.

The bid to establish a world record was billed as a sideshow but it dominated that year's World Conker Championship. Eamon's nearest rival was a Frenchman, who broke a paltry 42 conkers.

Freshford, Conker Capital of Ireland

THE VILLAGE SQUARE, FRESHFORD

A. Phelan '06

Hurling, Ireland's national game, is almost a religion in Kilkenny. Kilkenny have contested more All Ireland Hurling Finals than any other county and have been champions on 29 occasions, second only to Cork, with 30 titles. Kilkenny's black and amber jerseys are unique in that they are the only striped jerseys worn in the game of hurling.

The Holy Grail of hurling is the Liam McCarthy Cup which is presented to the winning All Ireland hurling team. The present cup (the original McCarthy Cup, purchased in 1922, was retired from wear and tear) was made by Kilkenny silversmith, James Mary Kelly, in 1992. It was first played for in that same year and was won by Kilkenny.

There have been many great Kilkenny hurlers down the years but perhaps the greatest form a trinity of their own: Lory Meagher (1899 – 1973) from Tullaroan who was aptly described as 'a hurling wizard' and in latter years Eddie Keher, from the Rower Inistioge, one of the greatest sharp-shooters in the game and finally D.J. Carey, from Gowran, who has been described as the greatest living hurler of his day.

Lory Meagher's homestead in Tullaroan, approx 19 km from Kilkenny, has now been turned into a GAA museum called Bród Tullaroan (*bród* meaning 'pride' in Irish). The 17th century, two-storey thatched cottage reflects the lifestyle of a well-to-do, farming family in the 19th century. A stone, purpose-built exhibition space, dedicated to Kilkenny's achievements in Gaelic games, was built within Bród Tullaroan Heritage Centre. The museum contains an interesting array of press-cuttings, photographs, trophies, old hurleys, sliothars, jerseys and other hurling memorabilia.

Nowlan Park, Kilkenny's county grounds, is called after Alderman James Nowlan, the longest serving ever GAA president. It was purchased in 1927 from Peter Corcoran of John Street for £700. It was agreed to impose a levy of £1 on each affiliated club to pay for equipment, and that the field be called Nowlan Park.

In recent years, Nowlan Park has been host, not just to the stars of hurling, but to such stars of the music world as Bob Dylan, Paul Simon, James Taylor, Rod Stewart and Andrea Boccelli, to mention but a few.

Hurling & Bród Tullaroan

LORY MEAGHER HOMESTEAD, TULLAROAN

The song *The Rose of Mooncoin* is Kilkenny's hurling anthem. The song, however, has nothing to do with hurling and is, in fact, a love song that tells of an impossible love affair between an ageing Catholic teacher and a young Protestant girl.

Watt Murphy was born in 1790 in the village of Rathkieran in south Kilkenny. His father Pat, a schoolteacher, taught in the nearby village of Ballyfoy. Watt Murphy eventually succeeded his father as teacher there.

In 1827 the wheat harvest was a disaster. As a result, around thirty families, unable to pay their rent, were evicted. Every building was levelled and almost overnight, Ballyfoy vanished from the map. Watt Murphy moved to nearby Polerone where he taught for five years.

He then moved to Mooncoin where he started his own private school in Chapel Street. A small, slightly bent man, he was known as 'The Rebel Poet'. Watt's school eventually came under the control of the parish, and when management problems led to Watt's dismissal, he returned to Polerone where a new vicar had been appointed.

Watt became quite friendly with Elizabeth Wills, the vicar's daughter. Despite their age difference – Elizabeth was barely twenty while Matt was fifty-six – they saw a lot of each other thanks to their mutual interest in poetry and music. At first Vicar Wills approved the relationship, believing his daughter to be a gentle companion for the lonely, aging teacher. Alarm bells rang, however, when Elizabeth declared her love for 'The Rebel Poet'. Age difference aside, they belonged to such different social and religious traditions that their union was doomed from the start.

Elizabeth's father immediately packed her off to London. With Elizabeth gone, Watt Murphy's world fell to pieces. He died of a broken heart in the 1850s but not before penning the poignant love song that has become the anthem of Kilkenny hurling, the love song in which Elizabeth, the vicar's daughter, becomes Molly, the famous Rose of Mooncoin.

'Oh Molly, dear Molly, it breaks my fond heart
To know that we two forever must part
I'll think of you, Molly, while sun and moon shine
On the banks of the Suir that flows down by Mooncoin'

In 1999, a monument was erected to Watt Murphy in the village of Mooncoin. That monument was unveiled by Kilkenny hurling legend: D.J. Carey.

The Rose of Mooncoin

THATCHED HOUSE, MAIN STREET, MOONCOIN

The people of Piltown call it 'The Tower', 'The Sham Tower' and 'Ponsonby's Tower'. The man who built it, however, didn't know what to call it. Not only that, he didn't quite know what to do with it and understandably so, when the story of Ponsonby's Tower is told.

It stands just outside Piltown, an unusual eight-sided building that immediately catches the eye. This rather lack-lustre monument bridges Piltown's past and present. It was built in the early 19th century by Lord Bessborough as a memorial to his son, Frederick Ponsonby, who, reportedly, was killed in the Napoleonic Wars. The grief-stricken Lord Bessborough decided to erect a monument to his son worthy of a soldier who had fallen in battle.

And then the unthinkable happened. The tower was half built when Frederick Ponsonby turned up at his father's estate in Piltown, alive and well. Lord Bessborough was obviously overjoyed at the return of his son whose 'death' was apparently due to a clerical error. But one small problem remained for Bessborough – what to do with the half built memorial to his son who was hale and hearty and taking his rightful place among the living of Piltown.

For reasons that we will never know, Lord Bessborough decided to do nothing. Construction of the monument ceased and a triangular cap-stone that was meant to be its crowning glory was abandoned in a local churchyard and can still be seen to this day.

And so the structure remained in limbo, an architectural oddity until the 1950s when the County Council converted it into a water tower. For three decades it served the community as a water tower until modernisation and progress rendered it idle once again.

To celebrate the millennium, a community group in Piltown decided, literally, to shine some light on the building by having it floodlit. And so it stands to this day, 'The Sham Tower', 'Ponsonby's Tower', part of Piltown's heritage – an unusual memorial to past and present.

Ponsonby's Tower, Piltown

A. PHELAN'07

Kilkenny has no coast-line yet the largest ship ever built on the shores of the river Suir was built by three Kilkenny men in Fiddown in south Kilkenny.

They called her 'The Titanic of Fiddown' and she was built by the Dwan brothers, Paddy, Jack and Jerry from Turkstown, a stone's throw from the quays of Fiddown.

It was the middle of the 19th century and the river Suir, like its sister rivers, the Nore and the Barrow, was a busy commercial highway. The Dwan brothers' boatbuilding expertise had earned them a reputation far and near. The Waterford boat builders, jealous of the brothers' reputation, challenged them to build a real, sea-going vessel.

In 1845 the brothers took up the challenge and decided to build the biggest ship ever seen in the Suir valley. From the four corners of Ireland people came to see the Dwan brothers at work. The project became something of a wonder throughout the country, so much so that the brothers christened the ship *The Wonder*.

After three years *The Wonder* was launched amidst great celebrations in the ancient south Kilkenny village. The 296 ton ship was a great success and enhanced the Dwan brothers' reputation. Although *The Wonder* was made to the highest level of care and craftsmanship it had one flaw – the mast was made of brittle larch, grown locally in the woods of Coolfin.

In 1851, around Easter time, the ship was returning home from a voyage. About thirty kilometres off the Waterford coast *The Wonder* was battered by a terrible storm. 'The Titanic of Fiddown' sank beneath the waves, bringing with it the three Dwan brothers and a cabin-boy from Dungarvan.

The boatyard of Fiddown no longer exists and boat-making skills have long vanished, however, *The Wonder* and the brothers who built it live on in local lore and memory.

'The Titanic of Fiddown'

THE BRIDGE AT FIDDOWN

On August 25th, 1769 James Agar was shot dead in a duel with Henry Flood at the triangle near Dunmore, a few kilometres outside Kilkenny.

The duel, apparently, was over a pair of pistols belonging to James Agar who claimed that Mr. Flood had them in his possession. The issue of the pistols (a convoluted story) would not normally lead to a duel but it brought to a head a bitter political feud between the Floods from Farmley, near Callan, and the Agars from Gowran.

The trouble began when the Agar family acquired the Manor of Callan and its surrounding lands, which had belonged to the Butlers of Ormonde but had been neglected by them over the years. The Floods from nearby Farmley had, more or less, claimed the neglected lands and had built up a substantial political base in Callan.

These two powerful families laid claim to the control of the Corporation of Callan. For the Agars, the claim was based on the property rights of Callan; for the Floods, the claim arose from continued and established usage.

On a number of occasions James Agar requested Flood to return his pistols but Flood denied any knowledge of them. On August 22nd 1769, the two men decided to settle matters at Dunmore.

According to an eyewitness account of the duel, James Agar fired first, shouting "Fire you scoundrel!", at Flood. Flood then fired, 'which shot inflicted a mortal wound over the left breast......a surgeon was immediately called for. I went to the place where Agar lay and saw Flood standing over him, Flood was very upset'.

Henry Flood was prosecuted for the murder of James Agar at Kilkenny Assizes on 13th April, 1770. As both seconds testified to the fair and honourable conduct of Henry Flood, he was fully acquitted of the charge. He went on to become a noted orator and a very prominent member of Grattan's Parliament.

James Agar had two sons and two daughters. George, his eldest son and heir was created Baron Callan, having been MP for Callan for many years.

Duel at Dunmore

THE CAVE BAR, DUNMORE

A.Phelan07

Callan in County Kilkenny is partially responsible for the success of one the world's most famous drinks, Coca Cola.

This story begins with an army officer, William Candler, who came to Ireland in 1649 with Oliver Cromwell. William Candler received large tracts of land in Wexford, Offaly and Kilkenny and he settled in Offaly.

William's second son, Thomas, an army officer also, moved to Callan where he lived in Callan Castle. Thomas and his wife Jane raised six children and it was his fourth son, Daniel, who set the Coca-Cola connection in motion.

Daniel fell madly in love with a local Catholic girl and much to his Protestant father's annoyance refused to give her up. His father duly disowned him but did, however, give Daniel enough money to emigrate to America where he and his wife Hanna became Quakers. We know this because one of Daniel's sons, William, became an officer in George Washington's army during the American War of Independence and had a biography written about him.

It was this William Candler's great grandson, Asa Candler, a pharmacist, who founded the Coca Cola Company in Atlanta, Georgia in 1892.

Coca Cola was created by the pharmacist, Dr. John S. Pemberton, in 1885, as a tonic for minor ailments. It was Pemberton's book-keeper, however, a man called Frank Robinson, who suggested the name Coca Cola and penned the now famous trademark in his unique script. Dr. Pemberton died in 1888 and over the next two years Coca Cola was acquired by the ambitious and dynamic Asa Candler, who became sole proprietor in 1891.

He became Mayor of Atlanta in 1916, and in 1919, Asa Candler, who had come to Atlanta with $1.50 in his pocket, sold the business for $25,000,000 – a phenomenal fortune at the time. He died in 1921, and his son Charles succeeded him as chairman of the Coca Cola company.

Asa and Charles Candler never forgot their Kilkenny roots and both built mansions in Atlanta, one called 'Callan Castle' and the other 'Callan Wolde'.

Coca Cola is still one of the most famous brands in the world – thanks to several generations of the Candler family, that old devil called love, Oliver Cromwell and the small town of Callan in County Kilkenny.

Callan and the Coca Cola Connection

ST. MARY'S CHURCH, CALLAN

A. Phelan '07

The word museum conjures up images of elegant, stately buildings that are usually state-funded. A little over six kilometres from Kilkenny city, on the outskirts of Bennetsbridge, is a museum that defies this description.

Seamus Lawlor's Folk and Farm Museum is unique in Ireland and possibly in Europe. The museum is the result of a lifetime's collecting by Seamus who opened it in the backyard of his house. The Nore Folk and Farm Museum is an Aladdin's cave of treasures from our past: thimbles, threshing machines, gramophones, grandfather clocks and an amazing array of agricultural gadgets, some dating back thousands of years.

The museum should have Saint Patrick as its patron as it was Seamus's involvement in exhibiting his historical acquisitions on the Saint Patrick's Day Parade floats that turned his hobby into an obsession.

When he retired from lorry-driving, Seamus dedicated his time and energy to the museum acquiring bits and pieces at auctions and car boot sales all over the south-east of Ireland. As the acquisitions accumulated, Seamus converted a large galvanised shed, at the rear of his house, into what is now the Nore Folk and Farm Museum. The year was 1993 and the museum is still going strong today.

A very popular exhibit is the replica of a rural pub from around the 1920s complete with beer barrels, old beer glasses and an old cash register to stash those old pounds, shillings and pence.

Another item of interest that many might not have heard of is the baby-cart. Buggies we are familiar with but this baby-cart was attached to a lady's bike, allowing the mother to transport the baby up hill and down dale.

Two exhibits in particular remind us of one of the darkest episodes in our history. One is the solid steel battering ram, used to evict starving tenants from their mud cabins during the Famine, and the other a very large wooden soup bowl used in soup-kitchens throughout the country to feed those dying from starvation.

The museum is open from 10 am to 6 pm on Saturdays and Sundays.

Bennetsbridge Folk & Farm Museum

OLD GARDA BARRACKS, BENNETSBRIDGE

A. Phelan 07

Inistioge is one of Kikenny's most picturesque villages. The rolling countryside and magnificent view of the river, with its eighteenth century bridge of nine arches, have delighted and captivated visitors down the years. In recent times Inistioge's beauty has captivated film directors, resulting in the making of two movies there *Circle of Friends* and *Widow's Peak*.

The village owes its foundation to the arrival of the Augustinian monks in 1220 AD. There are records, however, of a great battle there in which the men of Ossory defeated the Danes in 962 AD.

In 1650 another battle ensued with the arrival of Cromwell's troops The story goes that as they marched through the gates of Brownsford castle, expecting no opposition, the ladies of Inistioge ambushed them with beehives. The attack of the bumble-bees caused the Roundheads to beat a hasty retreat but only temporarily. In retaliation for the stinging attack, Colonel Axtel of the Cromwellian army had the Baron of Brownsford beheaded.

Inistioge is synonymous with the surrounding forest of Woodstock, and its magnificent walks, and with the Tighe family who lived at Woodstock House for about 150 years. The house was originally built in the 18th century for the family of Sir William Fownes. In 1793, Henry Tighe married his first cousin Mary Blanchford, who became known as Mary 'Psyche' Tighe because of a long poem she composed of the same title. Mary, a retiring, sensitive woman, died from TB at Woodstock in her 37th year.

Her tomb is in Inistioge's churchyard and contains a life-size, reclining statue of her created by the sculptor Flaxman.

Woodstock House with its panoramic views of the river Nore, was burned in July 1922 by anti-treaty forces. It had been the scene of splendid parties and political gatherings while its gardens, filled with rare plants and shrubs, were a haven for botanists and horticulturists and boasted the longest Monkey Puzzle walk in Europe. The gardens are presently being restored to their former glory and once again people can enjoy the charming, tree-lined walks.

Woodstock Heritage Museum, situated behind the village pump, houses an eclectic collection of photographs, documents, artefacts and memorabilia pertaining to the area.

Inistioge

THE VILLAGE SQUARE, INISTIOGE

H. Phelan '06

There are no less than three versions as to how Urlingford got its name. Owen O'Kelly in his book *The Place Names of County Kilkenny*, tells us that Urlingford comes from the Irish *Ath na nDóirling* meaning 'the ford of the big stones'.

Canon Carrigan in his *History and Antiquities of the Diocese of Ossory* writes of two other derivations: *Ath na nUrlaidhe* meaning: 'the ford of the sledgings', the name originating with a battle fought in the area in which *'the Irish and the Danes did sledge each other's heads'.* The more likely derivation, according to Carrigan, is *Ath na nUrlainn,* meaning 'the ford of the lawns or greens'.

Canon Carrigan also tells us that *'Urlingford is very modern, dating only from about 1775. In 1801 the town contained 176 houses, a distillery and a malt-house'.* In 1884, George Henry Bassett in his book *Kilkenny Guide and Directory* writes the following:

> *'Urlingford consists of one long street, the houses in which are nearly all thatched. The Bog of Allen skirts it and a small stream, called the Erkine, turns its only mill'. 'Urlingford',* he continues, *'has a patent for fairs, and holds six in each year, in this respect being very much ahead of Johnstown, which has a patent for eight fairs, and holds none'.*

Urlingford was once the venue for important hurling matches. In 1768 a match between Kilkenny and neighbouring Tipperary was attended by all the principal gentry who put up a prize of twenty guineas for the winners. Finn's Leinster Journal carried the following notice:

> *'The grand hurling match will go on next Sunday, 29th July 1768 for a wager of twenty guineas, at the Green of Quanthobus near Urlingford'.*

The Green of Quanthobus was located on the land now occupied by St. Joseph's Terrace. The story goes that at one of these encounters, as the Kilkenny team returned home, the Tipperary players threw stones at them, giving rise to Tipperary's nickname: 'the stone-throwers'. A few weeks later Munster played Leinster for a purse of sixty eight guineas. On 7th September 1768, the following appeared in Finn's *Leinster Journal*:

> *'The greatest hurling match that was ever hurled in Ireland will be played on Thursday 8th September between the provinces of Leinster and Munster for 68 guineas at the noted Green of Lisduff near Urlingford'.*

These old hurling matches were ferocious encounters and it was not unusual for lives to be lost. Perhaps there was some truth to the 'sledgings' version after all.

Urlingford

URLINGFORD LIBRARY

A. Phelan'07

Some Notable Kilkenny People

Like most Irish counties and towns, Kilkenny has its fair share of famous, and infamous, people. The following is a small, and personal, selection from Ye Faire Citie's catalogue of celebrities.

JAMES ARCHER

James Archer, after whom Archer's Avenue, Archer's Street and Archer's Court are called, was born in Kilkenny in 1550. A Jesuit and patriot, he was educated at Louvain in France, later in Rome and became the first Rector of the Irish College in Salamanca in Spain.

On his return to Ireland from Louvain, James Archer became a trusted ally of the great Hugh O'Neill and was a constant thorn in the side of the Crown. Actively involved in the counter-Reformation, he championed the Irish cause in Spain and drew down the wrath of the British Government.

This was a time of great religious tension in the country, so much so that in 1577, Sir William Drury, the Lord President of Munster reported that

'the students of Ireland that are in Louvain are the merest traitors and breeders of treachery that liveth". Drury went on to name James Archer from Kilkenny: "a detestable enemy to the Word of God'.

James Archer's audacity made him the stuff of legend throughout Ireland and he had so many escapes from the Crown that Sir William Drury said that he must have been helped by witchcraft.

Sometime after the disastrous Battle of Kinsale in 1601, James Archer returned to Spain where he continued to be a controversial figure. He spent the remainder of his life in Spain where he died on 15th February 1620 at the Irish college, Santiago Compostella. He was in his 70th year and was the oldest member of the Irish Jesuit Mission.

THE BANIM BROTHERS

The Banim brothers, John and Michael, were born in Kilkenny. Michael, a novelist in his own right, was born in 1796 and remained in Kilkenny all his life, giving up his legal ambitions to look after his father's hardware and gun shop.

John, born in 1798, studied art in Dublin and became a drawing master in St. John's College (Kilkenny College). He fell in love with one of his students which had tragic consequences. The young girl was removed from Kilkenny by her irate father and died of consumption. The despairing John Banim contracted spinal tuberculosis which would eventually kill him.

In 1820 John Banim returned to Dublin, abandoning art for literature. In 1822, he married a Miss Ruth and moved to London where he achieved success as a novelist and dramatist.

John and Michael Banim collaborated on a work that would bring their genius to the English literary world. Tales by the O'Hara Family reflected the lives of authentic Irish men and women as opposed to the hitherto clichéd stage Irishman. It is suggested that Michael supplied the raw material for John's literary talent from experiences gained behind his father's shop-counter in Kilkenny. The venture was an immediate success and *Tales by the O'Hara Family* was highly acclaimed in literary circles.

In 1835 John Banim moved to France on the advice of his doctors and was quite successful in Paris. However a series of misfortunes – the bankruptcy of his publisher, a severe attack of cholera, the death of his son from diphtheria and the death of his mother, to whom he was particularly devoted, together with his progressive paralysis – reduced him to a state of misery and dejection. His brother, Michael, alarmed at his condition begged him to come home.

In 1835, a broken man and unable to walk, John Banim, returned to Kilkenny where he received a warm welcome and was presented with an inscribed silver snuff-box containing £85. He received a Civil List pension of £150 per annum, and lived in Windgap Cottage on the Dublin Road with his wife. He died on August 4th 1842, aged 44 years. A bust of John Banim, by John Hogan, can be seen in Kilkenny's Tholsel in High Street.

Michael Banim, who was for some years postmaster and mayor of Kilkenny, retired to Booterstown, County Dublin where he died in 1874 aged 78. Both brothers are buried in Saint John's graveyard off Maudlin Street. Banim Terrace, in Kilkenny, is called after John and Michael Banim.

GEORGE BERKELEY

George Berkeley, Ireland's greatest philosopher, after whom Berkeley College in California is called, is credited with two birth places, one in Kilcreene on the outskirts of Kilkenny on 12th March, 1685 and the other at Dysart Castle in Thomastown where he spent his childhood. Educated in Kilkenny College, he later entered Trinity College in Dublin, graduating in 1704. He was ordained into the Church of Ireland in 1710.

Berkeley became an 'immaterialist', denying the existence of matter and arguing that things depended for their existence on being perceived *esse est percipi,* from the Latin, 'to be is to be perceived'. Among several works which established his reputation across Europe was his masterpiece *A Treatise Concerning the Principles of Human Knowledge* (1710).

Granted leave from his ministry in 1713, Berkeley quickly made his mark in the drawing rooms and coffee-houses of London. He became friendly with satirists, Pope and Swift and was, by all accounts, a most engaging character. A bishop Atterbury said of him:

"So much understanding, so much knowledge, so much innocence, and such humility I did not think had been the portion of any but angels till I saw this gentleman".

He later travelled extensively in France and Italy before returning to Dublin in 1721.

In 1724 he was appointed Dean of Derry and in 1728 he sailed for the New World, where he tried to establish a college in Bermuda to prepare colonists' sons for the ministry and to educate young American Indians. However, a promised government grant failed to materialise and he returned to England in 1731.

On his return to Ireland he was appointed to the bishopric of Cloyne, in Cork in 1734 where he spent seventeen years. During this time he wrote *The Querist,* a series of 595 questions about social and economic conditions in Ireland. It remains a prophetic and seminal piece of writing.

Life was difficult at Cloyne. There was sickness and disease but no doctors and no hospitals. Around 1740, deeply disturbed by the misery around him, Berkeley began his experiments with tar water, the curative powers of which he greatly believed in. In 1744 he published *Siris,* probably the best selling of his books, in which he described the virtues of tar water and provided descriptions of its manufacture and use. In July of 1752, in poor health, George Berkeley moved with his wife and daughter to Oxford to supervise his son George's university education. He died there in January 1753, in his 68th year.

CANON WILLIAM CARRIGAN

Few histories of Kilkenny and its environs (including this) are written without consulting Canon William Carrigan's *History and Antiquities of the Diocese of Ossory.* Canon Carrigan's magnus opus and labour of love is a godsend to all students of history, archaeology and genealogy in the Diocese of Ossory and beyond.

He was born in Ruthstown, Ballyfoyle, County Kilkenny in 1860, the youngest of a family of ten. His father, a reasonably well-off farmer, fostered an interest in antiquities and folklore, showing him how to decipher inscriptions in local graveyards.

Canon Carrigan taught Classics and English for two years in St. Kieran's College following his ordination by Bishop Moran in 1884. When he left St. Kieran's in 1886, he went on to serve in no less than five parishes. In 1890 Bishop Brownrigg suggested that he write a diocesan history because of his extensive knowledge of the diocese's past.

By the time he had settled down to write in 1897, he had walked every townland in the diocese. 'Fr. Willie', as he was affectionately known, mixed easily with the people, always gathering information about ancient churches and their patron saints, ruins and monuments, graveyards, holy wells, raths, moats and castles.

The actual writing of his history, with a quill pen and often by candlelight, took six years. In 1903 he was elected to the Royal Irish Academy and in 1905 his four-volume *History and Antiquities of the Diocese of Ossory* was published. In the midst of wide acclaim, however, he was severely criticised by a fellow priest in the diocese who published a 115 page booklet, entitled *Criticism of History and Antiquities of the Diocese of Ossory* by 'G.P.O.'. The booklet, a copy of which may be seen in Kilkenny's Carnegie Library on John's Quay, was more than likely motivated by personal spite.

Canon Carrigan lived austerely, setting little value on material things, and was noted for his generosity to the poor. He died in Durrow on the 12th December, 1924, aged 64, and is buried in Durrow chapel graveyard.

In 2005, to mark the centenary of the publication of the *History and Antiquities of the Diocese of Ossory,* a memorial garden was designed and planted beside Muckalee church by Mick Brennan – a distant relation of Canon Carrigan's mother, Johanna Brennan – and a committee comprising Billy Brett, Caroline Irwin, Paul Cochrane, Bernadette McCormack and Ron Butler.

Friar John Clyn

Friar John Clyn, born around 1300, was a contemporary of Dame Alice Kyteler, Kilkenny's famous witch, and Bishop Richard de Ledrede who tried her for witchcraft. A Franciscan, he resided in Saint Francis Abbey, the ruins of which still stand in the grounds of Smithwick's Brewery.

He was a diarist and an acute observer of events of the time. His writings are an invaluable record of contemporary life over a period of thirty three years from 1315 to 1348, and are an important source for Kilkenny's early historical records. He compiled diaries in Latin up until his death, when he fell

victim to the Black Death which ravaged Europe during the 14th century.

In 1334 he records the paving of the streets of Kilkenny, while in 1335 he notes the erection of the Market Cross, where many had the sign of the cross marked on their naked flesh with a red hot iron to ensure that they would be allowed go to the Holy Land.

Regarding the Black Death, or plague, of 1348 he writes:

'The pestilence was rife in Kilkenny in Lent. From Christmas Day to the 6th March eight friar preachers died off. Scarcely one alone ever died in a house. Commonly husband, wife, children and servants went the one way, the way of death.'

He writes also of *'agonising pains in the head and spittings of blood'* and says the plague was so contagious that *'anyone touching the dead or the sick was straight away infected and died so that penitent and confessor were often conveyed together to the grave'.*

The relentless spread of the Black Death, which wiped out almost half of the population of Europe, led Fr. Clyn to fear for the survival of mankind, as evidenced by the final entry in his diary,

'lest the writing should perish with the writer I leave parchment for continuing the work if happily any man survive, any of the race of Adam escape this pestilence and continue the work I have commenced'.

Friar John Clyn succumbed to the plague in 1349.

ABRAHAM COLLES

Abraham Colles, born at Millmount, Kilkenny in 1773, was the most outstanding Irish surgeon of the 19th century. The story goes that a flood in the river Nore severely damaged the house of a local doctor named Butler and swept a book of anatomy downstream where it was picked up by the young Colles in a meadow near his father's house. When he went to return the book, the doctor presented it to Colles and the incident is said to have had a significant influence on his choice of profession.

Educated in Kilkenny College, he later attended Trinity College, the Royal College of Surgeons and the Edinburgh School of Medicine. On his return to Ireland he became a member of the Royal College of Surgeons and in 1802 was elected president of the college at the age of twenty-nine.

He practiced his surgery in Dr. Steevens' Hospital in Dublin and performed pioneer operations without the assistance of anaesthetics (one wonders how the patients felt). In 1804 his academic ability was recognised by his appointment to the chair of anatomy and physiology and to the chair of surgery in the College of Surgeons.

A renowned teacher, he drew large crowds to his lectures and the college became so successful that it was necessary to extend the building on Saint Stephen's Green in 1825. Twice president of the Royal College of Surgeons, his name is familiar today in all hospitals because of the Colles' Fracture, an injury to the forearm, which he successfully identified and treated. The Colles Ward, in Dublin's Blackrock Clinic, is called after him.

Before his death he arranged that a post-mortem be carried out by Dr. Robert Smith. He thought it would be of benefit *'to ascertain by examination the exact seat of and nature of my last disease'.* Abraham Colles died in 1843 and the post-mortem, as requested, was performed by Dr. Smith.

CAPTAIN JAMES FRENEY

James Freney the Highwayman, known as Captain simply because he was leader of the gang, was born in Inistioge, County Kilkenny, in 1719. Kilkenny's own 'Robin Hood,' this most accomplished and likeable robber caused alarm and excitement in equal measures in the south-east of Ireland.

Small in stature, he contracted smallpox in 1745, aged 26, which left his face pock-marked and he also lost the sight in one eye. Losing one eye, however, did not diminish this small man's shooting abilities.

Freney treated highway robbery as a game and once robbed an army officer who was trying to capture him, in sight of his troop of soldiers. It is said that he never robbed a poor person, was always chivalrous towards the ladies and always left a gentleman enough money to get him to his destination.

He became a folk hero in his time and in 1748 negotiated a pardon for himself in return for which he informed on his partners in crime who were subsequently tried and hanged in Kilkenny in 1749. He published his autobiography in 1754. Whether it was written by himself or with the help of a hedge-school teacher, it proved to be a great success and *The Life and Adventures of James Freney* went to seven reprints, at least, over the next hundred years. The most recent edition (to the author's knowledge) was published in 1988 by Kilkenny writer Frank McEvoy with illustrations by local artist David Holohan.

James Freney obviously had influential friends as he was later employed as a customs official at New Ross Port, a post he held until his death in 1788 at the age of 69. He is buried in an unmarked grave in Inistioge, the heart of Freney country. Some of Captain James Freney's hoard is reputed to be buried on Brandon Hill in Graiguenamanagh. It has yet to be found.

James Hoban

James Hoban, the architect who designed the White House in Washington, was born in Desart Court near Callan, Co. Kilkenny in 1762, the same year as Edmund Ignatius Rice, the founder of the Christian Brothers. Having received some basic schooling he was apprenticed to a carpenter. When Lord Desart discovered that the young Hoban had outstanding abilities as an amateur architect he took him under his wing and had him formally trained at the Royal Dublin Society School under Thomas Ivory.

James Hoban excelled at his new profession and worked with some of the leading Irish architects of the time including James Gandon, architect of the Four Courts and the Custom House.

He emigrated to Philadelphia in 1781 where he continued his architectural career. He later moved to Washington which was nothing more than one long street with a population of no more than 1000 people. In 1792 Hoban took part in a competition, instigated by the US Congress, to design a 'Presidential Mansion'. He won the competition, a gold medal and $500. His winning entry, based on the design of Leinster House in Dublin, beat off a design put forward, anonymously, by Thomas Jefferson.

The corner stone of the 'Presidential Mansion' was laid in 1793 and the building was completed in 1801. It was damaged by fire in 1814 during the war between the United States and Britain (1812–1814). Hoban had the entire house painted white to cover up the indelible scorch marks, hence the name White House. The house, then fully restored, was opened in 1817.

In 1824 James Hoban designed Rosanarra House, a large country home, in Kilmoganny, near Callan, County Kilkenny. Sir John Lavery, the renowned portrait painter, lived his last years in Rosanarra, dying there in 1941. During the 1970s the American novelist, Richard Condon, author of *The Manchurian Candidate* and *Prizzi's Honour,* lived in Rosanarra for a while.

James Hoban became a very wealthy and influential member of Washington society. In addition to his architectural work, he was also a captain of the Washington Militia and a member of the City Council. He died in Washington on the 8th December 1831, aged 69 years.

MAEVE KYLE

Born in Kilkenny, Maeve Kyle made Irish sporting history when, in Melbourne in 1956, she became Ireland's first ever female athlete to compete in any Olympic games. A sprinter, she competed in the 100 metres and 200 metres.

Daughter of Corrodus Shankey, former headmaster of Kilkenny college, Maeve Kyle also excelled at hockey, winning 58 international caps including the Triple Crown triumph of 1958. She also competed in the 1960 Olympics in Rome and the 1964 Olympics in Tokyo where she reached the semi-finals of the 400 metres and 800 metres. Maeve Kyle now lives in Ballymena in County Antrim.

THE LARKIN FAMILY

The Larkin family from the Village (St. Patrick's parish) and the James Stephen's Hurling Club, hold a unique place in the annals of hurling and GAA history.

Three generations of the family, Paddy Larkin, his son Phil 'Fan' Larkin and 'Fan's son Philip, have played in no less than twenty two All Ireland senior hurling finals, winning eleven of them.

Paddy Larkin's hurling career started in St. Patrick's De La Salle primary school, as did 'Fan's' and Philip's. All three have served their club, James Stephen's, with great distinction, 'Fan' winning two All Ireland club championships, one in 1975, when he captained the team, and again in 1982, while son Philip won an All Ireland Club medal in 2004. However it's when it comes to the senior All Ireland Hurling Championship that they stake their claim to fame.

Paddy Larkin won his first All Ireland in 1932 against Clare, while a second followed in 1933 against Limerick. Two more All Ireland medals followed, one in 1935 and the last in the famous 'thunder and lightning final' of 1939 against Cork.

Phil 'Fan' Larkin won his first senior All Ireland medal in 1963 against Waterford. He won his second in 1972, with further honours coming in 1974, 1975 and 1979. 'Fan' continued to serve Kilkenny hurling as a selector and trainer of county senior, minor and under 21 teams, before taking up refereeing.

Philip Larkin was on two losing All Ireland teams, in 1998 and 1999, before winning his first All Ireland medal in 2000,

when Kilkenny brushed Offaly aside. This was a milestone for the Larkin family. Philip's medal meant that they were the first family in GAA history to win All Ireland honours across three generations.

Philip won his second All Ireland medal in 2002 and also won an All Star award creating further GAA history. 'Fan' Larkin and his son, Philip, became the first father/son combination to win All Star honours in the thirty-one year history of the awards – a feat that has yet to be emulated.

Tony O'Malley

Tony O'Malley, one of Ireland's foremost painters, was born in Bridge Street, Callan in 1913. His father, Patrick O'Malley, a Clare Island man, was a travelling salesman for Singer sewing machines. His mother, local girl Margaret Ryan, ran a small shop and at one time a lending library.

Tony O'Malley attended school in the Convent of Mercy primary school and the CBS in West Street, Callan. He worked for the Munster and Leinster Bank from 1933 to 1958, serving in many branches nationwide. He joined the Irish Army during the Emergency but was discharged a year later in 1941 due to ill health. During his four years in the Kilkenny sanatorium with TB, Tony drew and painted every day, developing his skill and technique. In 1951 he was discharged as fully cured and returned to work in the bank.

Tony had received no formal art training but had an overwhelming need to paint. Some of his earliest work depicts local scenes of Callan, including sketches of The King's river.

*'What was I? I asked myself: what am I? And I
had to say: I am only the person who wants to go
down the King's river and make a drawing of the
river there … That's what I am. I had to speak to
myself and answer to myself: I am only this'.*

Tony O'Malley (from *Tony O'Malley*, edited by Brian Lynch)

In 1960, he took the brave step of turning his back on a secure job and moved to the artists' colony in St. Ives in Cornwall, where he could devote all his time to painting. There he met Canadian artist Jane Harris, from Montreal, whom he married in 1973. They regularly travelled to Lanzarote and the Bahamas, where the light and colour had a huge influence on his work. In 1990 they settled permanently in Physicianstown in Callan.

In 1981 Tony O'Malley was elected to Aosdana. In 1989 he was made an honorary member of the Royal Hibernian Academy and in 1994, Trinity College conferred an honorary doctorate on him. In the same year the then President of Ireland, Mary Robinson, invested Tony O'Malley with the Torc, the necklet symbolic of his election by members of Aosdana as a Saoi. The previous wearer of this Torc was the writer and Nobel Prize winner, Samuel Beckett. On 11th February 2000, Tony O'Malley was made a freeman of Kilkenny city in recognition of his artistic achievements, the only Callan man to receive such an honour. He died on 20th January, 2003.

EDMUND IGNATIUS RICE

Edmund Ignatius Rice, the founder of the Irish Christian Brothers, was born at Westcourt in Callan in 1762. Son of a prosperous Catholic farmer, his wife was killed in a riding accident in 1789. They had been married only two years. The tragic death of his wife drew Edmund Rice closer to God and he became more involved in his work with the poor and underprivileged.

A successful business man, he inherited his uncle's business in 1794. In 1802 he opened a school for underprivileged boys in a stable in New Street, Waterford. As the school grew, he was joined by two young volunteers from Callan to help with the education of these boys. He withdrew from business and his privileged lifestyle and lived an austere life in humble accommodation. Edmund Rice went on to build a monastery, Mount Sion, on the outskirts of Waterford, setting up a bake-house to feed the poor and hungry pupils.

Additional schools were opened as Edmund Rice and his companions adapted rules from the Presentation nuns. Dressed in a monk's robe, he called himself Brother Ignatius. In 1817 Edmund Rice sought papal approval for a constitution under which all his foundations would be amalgamated with one superior general. Five years later, in 1822, he was elected Superior General of the Christian Brothers.

In 1824 the following statement was put before the British House of Parliament:

"In the town of Waterford there is one who has devoted his time in a most praiseworthy manner to the benevolent purpose of educating the ignorant and destitute part of his countrymen. I never saw more order, more regularity or greater system, than in that school under the superintendence of Mr. Rice".

When he retired in 1838, the Christian Brothers order had seventeen houses and forty-three schools. Edmund Ignatius Rice died at Mount Sion, Waterford on 29th August, 1844 aged 82 years. Blessed Edmund Ignatius Rice was beatified in Rome by Pope John Paul II on 6th October 1996. The thatched house where he was born has been restored and is now the Edmund Rice Heritage Centre in Westcourt, Callan.

JAMES STEPHENS

James Stephens, the founder of the Irish Republican Brotherhood (the IRB), was born in Kilkenny in 1824. Educated in St. Kieran's College, he became a railway engineer. In 1848 he was part of the abortive Young Ireland rising, led by William Smith O'Brien, which began and ended with a skirmish with police in Ballingarry, County Tipperary. Wounded in the thigh, he escaped to Paris, while back in Kilkenny, his friends pretended he had died and staged his funeral by burying a stone-filled coffin. In Paris, Stephens earned a living from teaching and journalism but was always plotting revolution with John O'Mahoney, another survivor from Ballingarry.

When he returned home, Stephens travelled thousands of miles around Ireland, assessing the prospects of establishing a secret movement. This earned him the nickname *An Seabhac Siúlach* – 'the Roaming Hawk'. He founded the IRB on Saint Patrick's Day, 1858. At the same time, in America, his associate John O'Mahoney founded its counterpart, The Fenians, the name by which the whole organisation became popularly known. In 1863 James Stephens launched a republican news-paper *The Irish People.* Stephens fell out with O'Mahoney and the American wing of the organisation because of his dictatorial attitude. He lived in Paris again for a period before returning to Dublin, where he spent his life in seclusion and died in 1901. James Stephens gave his name to Kilkenny's swimming pool and to James Stephen's Hurling Club in Saint Patrick's parish, also known as The Village. John Bolger, former mayor of Kilkenny, lives in the house where James Stephens was born in Blackmill Street.

GODWIN MEADE SWIFTE

In 1856, almost half a century before the Wright brothers made aviation history at Kitty Hawk, Carolina, a Kilkenny-born man by the name of Godwin Meade Pratt Swifte, the second Viscount of Carlingford, built what he called an Aerial Chariot. He built the machine in the dining room of his home, Swiftsheath, an elegant country house in Jenkinstown, where Jonathan Swift, the author of *Gulliver's Travels* purportedly spent some of his childhood. The doorway of the dining room had to be enlarged to allow the machine to be wheeled in and out and this 'extension' can be viewed to this day.

Lord Carlingford patented his Aerial Chariot in Dublin and this patent, No 2993, along with the propellers and a screw from the Aerial Chariot,can be seen in Rothe House Museum, in Parliament St., Kilkenny. The patent is an interesting document which seems to contain principles and details then new to aviation. The 'Apparatus for Navigating the Air', as Lord Carlingford sometimes referred to it, was towed by horses to Foulksrath Castle, now a youth hostel, near Swiftsheath. It was hauled to the summit, where, with his butler at the controls, Lord Carlingford 'propelled him forth'. Unfortunately it crashed and the butler broke his leg. He duly received a pension for life in compensation (or so the story goes).

Lord Carlingford himself was a colourful character, to say the least. A diplomat in Venice, he once brought his private gondola, complete with a team of gondoliers dressed in scarlet and gold, to London. The gondola was mounted on a dray, and with the gondoliers going through the motions of rowing, was pulled by ten horses all the way to Buckingham Palace, where a formal reception was being held. He was also responsible for the ancient spelling of his family name – using the final letter e. As eccentric a character as Lord Carlingford was, he did design and construct a heavier-than-air flying machine. Although the Aerial Chariot crashed on its first outing there are reports that for a few fleeting moments it actually did fly, which would mean that a Kilkenny man, a humble butler, was the first person to fly, all of fifty years before the famous Wright brothers!

Bibliography

Bradley, John, *Discover Kilkenny,* O'Brien Press, 2000

Cahill, John, *100 Years of Hurling in Urlingford,* 2007

Carrigan, Canon, *History and Antiquities of the Diocese of Ossory*

Coakley, Davis, *Irish Masters of Medicine,* Townhouse, 1992

Doyle, J., *Glimpses of Kilkenny in the 18th century,* 1983

Fitzgerald, John, *Kilkenny City & County, People, Places, Faces,* Callan Press

Jackson, Robert Wyse, *The Story of Kilkenny,* Mercier Press, 1974

Kenny, Claire, *Talbot's Inch, The Origins of Kilkenny's Model Village,* 1989

Kenny, Sean, *Every Stick and Stone that Stands Kilkenny,* Kilkenny People Printing, 2003

Niely, W. G., *Kilkenny an Urban History, 1391 – 1843,* The Institute of Irish Studies, The Queen's University, Belfast 1989

Nolan, William, and Whelan, Kevin, Eds., *Kilkenny, History and Society,* Geography Publications, 1990.

O'Carroll, Joseph, *Historic Kilkenny,* 1994

O'Kelly, Owen, *The Place-Names of County Kilkenny,* The Kilkenny Archaeological Society and Mrs. Sheila O'Kelly, 1985

Phelan, Margaret M., *St. Mary's Cathedral, Notes on its Foundation, Construction and Furnishings,* 1972.

Smith, Albert, *A Brief History of Kells, Co. Kilkenny,* Published by KRETE, 1993

Sparks, May, *Inns and Taverns of Old Kilkenny,*

Tynan, Pat, *Kilkenny, History & Guide,* Nonsuch Publishing 2006

Wallace, Martin, *Famous Irish Lives,* Appletree Guides, 1991

Walsh, Joe and Seamus, *In the Shadow of the Mines,* 1999

Winn, Christopher, *I Never Knew That About Ireland,* Ebury Press, 2006

Woods, Macdara Ed., *The Kilkenny Anthology,* Kilkenny County Council, 1991

Callan, A Short Guide to its History, Monuments & People, Callan Heritage Society, 2000

Kilkenny City and County, Guide and Directory (Facsimile Edition), Grangesilvia Publications, Kilkenny, 2001

Kilkenny Design, Twenty One years of Design in Ireland, Kilkenny Design Workshops, 1984

Old Kilkenny Reviews, Journals of Kilkenny Archaeological Society

Dear Reader
This book is from our much complimented illustrated book series which includes:-

We can also supply prints, individually signed by the artist, of the paintings featured in many of the above titles as well as many other areas of Ireland.

For the more athletically minded our illustrated walking book series includes:-

We have an exciting new range of books which covers rivers in Ireland:-

Cottage
Publications

Cottage Publications
is an imprint of
Laurel Cottage Ltd
15 Ballyhay Road
Donaghadee, Co. Down
N. Ireland, BT21 0NG

For details on these superb publications and to view samples of the paintings they contain, you can visit our web site
www.cottage-publications.com
or alternatively you can contact us as follows:–
Telephone: +44 (0)28 9188 8033
Fax: +44 (0)28 9188 8063